Perspectives on Environmental Conflict and International Politics

TAPRI STUDIES IN INTERNATIONAL RELATIONS

This series, edited jointly by Dr Vilho Harle and Dr Jyrki Käkönen of the Tampere Peace Research Institute (TAPRI) at Tampere in Finland, is based on the work of TAPRI on peace studies. The series is launched with publications from TAPRI Workshops on European Futures: Bases & Choices. The workshops have concentrated on European issues concerning international relations, security, disarmament, human rights, technology and co-operation.

List of publications:

Vilho Harle and Pekka Sivonen (eds), *Europe in Transition: Politics and Nuclear Security*

Vilho Harle (ed.), *European Values in International Relations*

Vilho Harle and Jyrki Iivonen (eds), *Gorbachev and Europe*

Allan Rosas and Jan Helgesen (eds), *Human Rights in a Changing East/West Perspective*

Vilho Harle and Pekka Sivonen (eds), *Nuclear Weapons in a Changing Europe*

Perspectives on Environmental Conflict and International Relations

Edited by Jyrki Käkönen

Pinter Publishers
London and New York

© Tampere Peace Research Institute 1992

First published in Great Britain in 1992 by
Pinter Publishers Limited
25 Floral Street, London WC2E 9DS

British Library Cataloguing in Publication Data
A CIP catalogue record for this book is available from the
British Library

ISBN 1 85567 0194

Library of Congress Cataloging-in-Publication Data
Perspectives on environmental conflict and international politics /
    edited by Jyrki Käkönen.
        p.   cm.—(TAPRI studies in international relations)
    Includes bibliographical references and index.
    ISBN 1-85567-019-4
    1. Economic development—Environmental aspects.   2. Natural
resources—Management.   3. International economic relations.
I. Käkönen, Jyrki.   II. Series.
HD75.6.P48   1992   91–30841
363.7'056—dc 20   CIP
ᵗᴾ

Typeset by Florencetype Ltd, Kewstoke, Avon
Printed in Great Britain by Biddles Ltd

Contents

Contributors

MATTHIAS FINGER, PhD in Adult Education (University of Geneva, 1986); PhD in Political Science (University of Geneva, 1987); Visiting Assistant Professor, Syracuse University (1989–); various visiting academic positions in Switzerland, France, Finland and Canada. Current main interest: political and social implications of global environmental crisis.

JUDIT GALAMBOS, MA Studies: University of Economics, Budapest (1978–1983); Bologna Center of the Johns Hopkins University, School of Advanced International Studies, Bologna (1983–1984). Work: Research Fellow, Hungarian Institute of International Affairs (1983–1990); from 1990: Associate to the Program Manager, Regional Environmental Center for Central and Eastern Europe, Budapest. Current main interest: management of environmental conflicts, public participation in decisions concerning the environment.

LASSI HEININEN, Licentiate in Political Science (University of Tampere, Finland, 1991); Research Fellow at Tampere Peace Research Institute (1990–). Edited a report: 'Arctic Environmental Problems' (Tampere Peace Research Institute, 1990).

JYRKI KÄKÖNEN, PhD in Political Science (University of Turku, Finland, 1986); Director of Tampere Peace Research Institute (1988–). Most recent book: *National Resources and Conflicts in the Changing International System: Three Studies on Imperialism* (Avebury, 1988).

TUOMO MELASUO, Licentiate in Political Science (University of Turku, Finland, 1981); Research Fellow at Tampere Peace Research Institute (1985–). Edited: *National Movements and World Peace* (Avebury, 1990).

M.A. MOHAMED SALIH, PhD (University of Manchester, 1983); Senior Researcher at the Scandinavian Institute of African Studies (1987–). Edited: *Ecology and Politics in Africa* (Scandinavian Institute of African Studies, 1989).

RICHARD MOOREHEAD, MA in African Studies (University of

Sussex); Economist, Director IUCN Project for the Conservation of Nature in the Inland Niger Delta 1984–8. Writing doctorate at the Institute of Development Studies, University of Sussex (1988); current main interest: common property management systems and the environment.

MARVIN S. SOROOS, PhD in Political Science (Northwestern University, 1971); Professor and Department Head, North Carolina State University (1970–). Most recent book: *Beyond Sovereignty: the Challenge of Global Policy* (University of South Carolina Press, 1986).

TAPANI VAAHTORANTA, BA Politics (University of Turku, 1980); MA in Politics (Princeton University, 1985); Director, The Finnish Institute of International Affairs, Helsinki (1991–). Main interest: international environmental politics.

1 Introduction

Jyrki Käkönen

Environmental problems have occupied an important position in peace research since the late 1980s and there are at least two major reasons for their predominance:

1. Modern peace research was established in order to prevent any kind of nuclear war. A possible nuclear war was seen as a threat towards the whole of human civilization.

   In the late 1980s it became clear that nuclear war would be impossible. It is true that as long as there are nuclear weapons there is also an opportunity for nuclear war, but the changes in Europe in 1989 and the ending of the Cold War made a nuclear war less realistic than hitherto.

   At the same time the awareness of environmental catastrophe has increased. Environmental problems have taken the place of nuclear weapons as a source of anxiety. People have begun to understand that environmental problems can also totally destroy human civilization. The Brundtland Commission's report gave only 20 years for the solving of the main environmental problems. After that there will be very little to be done.

2. It has become clear that environmental problems are not neutral by nature. Environmental changes like pollution create conflicts between different social or ethnic groups within a single state and also between different states. Since these conflicts are potential sources for open violence it follows that environmental problems or environmental conflicts traditionally belong to the sphere of peace research. Therefore, in peace research environmental problems have been seen as social rather than ecological problems. They are even of a political nature.

It is possible to present environmental problems as a manifestation of the crisis of the so-called modernization project, as Finger argues in his chapter in this book. From the late fifteenth century up to the present, humanity has moved towards a centralized and unified world system. Many factors have harmonized the structure. The simultaneous existence of different social models has not changed the tendency towards harmonization. In different social systems the means of attaining economic growth and increasing the material standard of living have been different, but the aims have been the same.

The creation of one world system and its increasing integration have destroyed true regionalism and local cultures. In the historical process of modernization the role of local or traditional cultures has been underestimated. Cultures have been codes by which human societies have adapted themselves to different geographical and natural conditions. In the making of the world system, local cultures have been destroyed and the capacity to adapt to different conditions is disappearing. With modernization the environment has been utilized for profit and the sustainability of the environment has become less important.

In this book we have tried to show how traditional cultures and modes of production have been able to adapt to their environments; people have organized themselves socially in order to utilize their environment in a sustainable way (see the chapters by Moorehead, Mohamed Salih and Melasuo). When we speak of sustainable development today, we should remember the connection between local culture and sustainable development.

It is possible to read history in such a way that modernization and construction of the so-called nation-states are seen to have moved the decision-making on the use of the environment away from the local level where practical utilization always occurs. At the same time more effective and profitable utilization has been called for. This has increased ecological stress. It has also destroyed local ability to adapt to the environment. Politically it has meant that local people, minorities in the state systems and in the world system, have been deprived of their self-managing capacity. Political power has moved from local to state level. The so-called nation-state has replaced civil society.

This historical transformation process has given rise to antagonistic interests represented by different social, political and economic entities. The possibility of conflict has grown, for instance between local and distant national interests, indigenous people and newcomers, poor and rich, and traditional and modern factors. These social contradictions make environmental conflicts political.

The above argument leads to the question whether we must return to local autonomy and traditional cultures and modes of production in order to solve environmental problems. In posing this question I accept the view that environmental conflicts are not specific to any social formation and that they are expressions of criticism of modernization, as is demonstrated by the chapters by Heininen and Galambos. However, it must be stressed that some traditional cultures have also caused environmental problems; some have even been destroyed by overutilizing their environment. Therefore, environmental problems force one to take a critical attitude towards the growth-oriented modernization project.

There is an increasing awareness of environmental problems. At the same time, however, very limited attention has been paid to growth and modernization, which are obviously basic factors in our current environmental problems. In politics, growth orientation is still essential. It is possible to think that on the systemic level we are not ready or able to choose any alternative to growth-oriented modernization. It is difficult to turn the current of history. Since this seems to be inevitable, the contradiction between the poor South and the rich North increases. Environmental problems will be most critical in the less developed societies. In poor countries people have to survive and they can have little thought for the environment.

Consciousness of environmental problems will give rise to further difficulties for the developing world. The EC, and other developed economies, will create environmental standards to protect vulnerable nature. This means that there will be environmental standards for products, and at the same time strict limits on the use of airplanes. This kind of restriction means that fewer products from the developing world will reach the markets of developed societies. And planes of Third World airlines do not fly to the developed countries. Third World countries do not have enough capital for the technology which would save the environment.

The above arguments mean that poor societies will ultimately pay the cost of protecting the environment. Environmental problems will become a weapon against less developed countries. This leads to a situation where we have environmental refugees from the Third World knocking on our doors in Europe and North America. Poverty and environmental destruction go hand in hand, as do wealth and the resources to take care of the environment. This will be the case as long as we are unwilling to change our values, from which our problems spring.

Within this framework, environmental conflict is first of all a conflict between state and civil society, a conflict in which power elites express the interests of the state, while there is no forum for the interests of civil society. By organizing itself into movements civil society can express its interests and set them against those of the centralized state. If civil society can organize itself into a forum of self-management there is no need for a romantic return to the past. The environmental problem can probably be solved in the context of the modernization project, as Soroos and Vaahtoranta suggest in their chapters. On the other hand, Finger levels sharp criticism at this kind of optimism.

Finally, I would like to say that civil society has to manifest the environmental conflict as a social conflict of interests. According to conflict theories, only manifested conflicts can be solved. As long as we see environmental problems as neutral and related simply to the condition of nature, there are few real possibilities for solving them. Environmental conflicts need political solutions.

In the Tampere Peace Research Institute (TAPRI) environmental problems have found their place and they will play a large part in the institute's forthcoming research orientation—as has been demonstrated by the organization of a seminar on 'Environmental conflicts'. The seminar was a part of the international TAPRI workshops on 'European futures: Bases and choices' held in Orivesi, Finland on 10–12 October 1989. The TAPRI workshops were financed mainly by a grant from the John D. and Catherine T. MacArthur Foundation, to whom we would express our warmest thanks.

This book is based on the papers presented to that seminar. Knowing that the aim of TAPRI is to deal with environmental problems as social and political issues, we would like to say that in environmental problems there is great potential for conflict. The role of peace research is to spell this out and to try to find peaceful solutions. In Chapter 2 Mathias Finger tries to find a place for environmental issues in peace research. In Chapter 3, Marvin Soroos describes how environmental issues influence international politics and points to the need to create a climate for cooperation. In Chapter 4 Tapani Vaahtoranta continues the discussion on international cooperation, especially in the area of air pollution.

In the next three chapters the authors deal with different aspects of water pollution: Lassi Heininen points out that the naval presence in Arctic waters is a threat to the marine environment; Judit Galambos describes a transnational conflict in connection with water construction; and Richard Moorehead shows that modernization makes the traditional multiform use of a changing water area difficult, if not impossible. All this leads to conflict: M. Mohamed Salih and Tuomo Melasuo analyze the conflict caused by different forms of using land in Sudan and in Ethiopia. In the final chapter I discuss a comprehensive concept of security. I do this in order to show that the political struggle has to take its place in the reallocation of social capital for different social purposes.

2 New Horizons for Peace Research: The Global Environment[1]

Mathias Finger

Peace researchers are increasingly realizing that there are other global urgencies beyond the global nuclear threat. Global changes—in particular climatic changes—are probably inevitable. Even the drastic measures we could take now would already be too late. Many of these measures would seriously affect our living standard (energy savings, more efficient technology), but unfortunately they will not be enough.

We are more and more aware of this, but at the same time we also realize, perhaps even more so than in the case of the nuclear threat, that there is a certain helplessness among the major actors of modern society. This general helplessness has philosophical and epistemological roots, which were well known in the 1970s, but by now mostly forgotten. Nevertheless, it can be argued that today's global ecological crisis is epistemologically linked to the nature of modernization itself, i.e. to the very nature of the extraordinary dynamics of our Western civilization.

Forgetting this, we might simply cure symptoms instead of looking into the causes of the crisis. If we consider that at least some of today's global ecological problems stem from the very nature of modernity— i.e. the industrial (techno-economic) revolution, the French (political) revolution, the scientific revolution of the Renaissance, and possibly even to Judaeo-Christianity and Greek philosophy—then it becomes understandable why it is so difficult to come up with solid alternatives. It also becomes understandable that such alternatives will have to have a (new) cultural basis. But no such alternative framework— though badly needed as a new perspective which could inspire the citizen to strive again for a new collective project—is today in sight. Only in the context of a new cultural perspective will epistemological alternatives to industrial development, to technological science and to nation-state power politics become thinkable again. Peace researchers could significantly contribute to this thinking by considering the 'weapons culture' as an expression of today's global crisis.

As military issues more and more give way to ecological issues, peace researchers should become acquainted with, but also look critically at the new emerging trend toward global environmental management. This chapter aims at providing a critical introduction to a field too long neglected by peace research.

1. A short history of ecology as a socio-cultural phenomenon

In order to understand the very nature, as well as the various functions, of today's new trends toward global environmental management, it is useful to have a look into the history of political ecology (see, e.g., Grinevald, 1987a).

1.1 Political ecology of the 1970s

Very little has been written on the origins of political ecology in the 1970s; in fact, a theory explaining the emergence of ecological issues and concern in the late 1960s is still lacking. Nevertheless, one explanatory factor—though in itself not a sufficient one—is the countercultural movement of the 1960s in the United States and the more political movement of May 1968 in Europe. The emergence of ecology as a socio-cultural phenomenon has to be located within the context of these social and political movements, and this is the reason why, today, we speak of this ecology of the 1970s as 'political ecology'. This does not mean that the political conception of this movement must be considered a solution; rather, history has shown the opposite, as one can see from the Russian and the Chinese examples. But what seems important here is that the ecological movement of the 1970s did ask political questions.

The promoters of this political ecology are/were social and political movements, as well as socially and politically concerned citizens. The intellectuals, the writers, and others who have done most of the thinking and the theorizing for this political ecology are/were always 'dissidents of the system'. Consequently, the stress in their analysis is on the political, as well as on the socio-economic dimensions of the ecological crisis, which is always also a crisis of the 'system'.

Grinevald (1984) has in a substantial bibliography monitored the evolution of ecological concern, issues and thinking since World War II. His data show an 'explosion' of political ecology in the 1970s around such crucial issues as chemical, nuclear, or more generally industrial pollution. Other equally crucial and global issues of political ecology are militarization, but also scientific and technological development, as well as extinction, and indeed industrial civilization as such. Even the origins of peace research can be located within this political ecology movement.

For all these thinkers the ecological crisis appears to be a crisis of Western civilization. Therefore, they all place the stress on the philosophical, the anthropological and, most important, the epistemological or rather the socio-epistemological roots of the ecological crisis. Such thinking was mostly unprecedented and has hardly been pursued since the decline of the movement in the early 1980s, or rather its transformation into new forms of ecology.

1.2 *Global ecology/environment in the 1980s*

One of the key differences between the ecology of the 1970s and that of the 1980s is its relation to politics. Political ecology in the 1970s had in fact a difficult but nevertheless rich relation to politics, which was seen as part and parcel of the ecological crisis. Political reforms/ revolutions were considered necessary to get at the very roots of ecological problems. In other words, ecological movements sought not only an answer to ecological problems, but also a transformation of the (political) 'system'. This is totally different from today's trend toward global environmental management: the new trend considers politics as a simple means to solve environmental problems; policies become management tools. It will later be argued that this is a naive conception of politics, which, at least partly, can be explained by an undifferentiated analysis of the socio-political and cultural roots of today's environmental crisis.

Again, however, we lack a historical understanding of the socio-cultural origins of the new trends. What is clear, on the other hand, is that global environmental management no longer has anything to do with the social and political movements of the 1970s. Rather, the opposite is the case: it may equally well be the expression of a weakening of these very movements. As I will show, this new trend neglects the social, political and economic aspects of the new global ecological/ environmental issues, as well as voiding them in the philosophical, anthropological and (socio-) epistemological considerations of the 1970s. Moreover, it disregards the traditional actors of political ecology (the concerned citizens, grassroots activists, local associations and movements, volunteer organizations, etc.), to count only on (political) management strategies. This is again to show how much concern for the global ecology/environment is a fundamentally new trend.

It must be noted that, historically, this new trend is in fact of two different origins, which make for a difference between 'global ecology' and 'global environmental management'. Global ecology refers to the scientific dimension of the new trend, and moreover to a rather neglected type of natural science, which also has nothing to do with the traditional scientific ecology of the 1970s. If the traditional scientific ecology refers to the dominant scientific epistemology of the 'infinitely small' (nuclear physics, analytical chemistry and micro-biology), the new global ecology focuses on the Earth and atmospheric sciences, whose points of reference are extensive and long-term cycles.

Global environmental management, on the other hand, refers to the political dimension of this new trend. As such, it can be traced back to the political ecology of the 1970s, or rather to a recuperation of it. The origin of 'global environmental management' is certainly the year 1972, i.e. the Stockholm Conference on the Human Environment, as well as the first report to the Club of Rome (Meadows et al., 1972). Ever since, the idea of 'global environmental management' has been promoted by institutions such as the Club of Rome, the United Nations Environment Program, 'Global 2000', the report to President Carter (Barney, 1980) and others.

At the beginning of the 1980s the idea of 'global environmental management' gained considerable (scientific) support from the now emerging trend to global (scientific) ecology. Since that time, global ecology and global environmental management, though promoted by different types of actors, talk about the same kind of global issues and imagine the same kind of solutions to them. They can therefore be considered as two parts of the same new global trend, to which one can address similar critiques. Nevertheless, both trends should be distinguished in what concerns their 'knowledge interest', as well as their socio-political implications and their socio-cultural significance.

2. New global issues

The traditional issues of political ecology of the 1970s were mainly concerned with concrete industrial pollution as well as the physical degradation of nature by industrial projects and urbanization. Concern for such issues arises from 'bottom up'; this means it is stirred up at a grassroots and local level, mainly by actors who are themselves personally concerned. Traditionally, actions to protect the environment are therefore a result of ecological groups, associations and movements putting pressure mainly on the political system of the nation-states. These actions are usually accompanied by political, and more generally, philosophical considerations defining what is politically and socially good and desirable.

Today, and over the last two to three years, a totally different trend has been gaining ground. This trend pertains to what Clark and Holling (1985) call 'third-generation concern', as opposed to first- and second-generation concern. I cannot agree with their way of writing the history of ecology, since according to them the concerns differ only in scale. The present text is based on the idea that there is a profound difference between different concerns, a difference in terms of issues, actors, epistemological conceptions and ways of conceiving socio-political transformation. The new (third-generation) issues take the form of a disturbance of global bio-geo-chemical cycles, of climate change and of geosphere-biosphere modelling. They are raised by a special category of scientists (some professional ecologists, but mainly geochemists, climatologists and atmospheric experts), taken up by a new category of experts we could call 'global managers', and brought to public awareness in top–down manner through massive media campaigns.

Let us briefly present the most important global epistemological issues, as seen by the World Watch Institute (Brown and Flavin, 1988, p. 3):

The earth's forests are shrinking, its deserts expanding, and soils eroding—all at record rates. Each year thousands of plant and animal species disappear, many before they are named or catalogued. The ozone layer in the upper atmosphere that protects us from ultraviolet radiation is thinning. The very temperature of the earth appears to be rising, posing a threat of unknown dimension to virtually all life support systems on which humanity depends.

Some of these phenomena were already known in the 1970s, but as local problems, whereas others, like the warming up of the climate and consequent sea level rise, are new. What is typically new in the 1980s, however, is that first, these phenomena now appear on a global level with global effects, and second, most of them interact and reinforce each other. This synergetic global effect must be considered one of the most important discoveries of global ecology.

Indeed, the core of the new global ecological issues are the bio-geo-chemical cycles and their interactions. They are as cycles increasingly disturbed by human activities; in fact, one should understand economic and industrial activities. The picture one gets (mainly from the media) is that of Earth as a more and more fragile eco-system, which has not only to be protected, but moreover wisely managed.

3. New modes of socio-political transformation?

Never before have the media, and under their pressure some politicians, paid so much attention to ecology. Far more concrete and immediate threats, such as potential nuclear and chemical accidents—be they military or civil—did not receive comparable attention. In my opinion, this cannot be explained solely by the scope of the ecological threats and by their urgency. Another, complementary, explanation of recent media attention to these threats lies in the epistemological nature of the new global issues. Therefore, the relation of global ecology to politics is fundamentally different. Global ecology does not threaten but reinforces existing political structures; it does not threaten but reinforces big science and 'science-fueled' technological progress. Unlike the (political) ecological issues of the 1970s, which were highlighted by social and political movements, and which aimed at political transformation, the new global issues are highlighted by scientifically legitimated experts, who seek to use politics (and probably also the media) as a simple tool for global environmental management.

A look at the cultural context of the 1980s helps to understand this new conception of socio-political transformation. The new ecological issues arise in a new cultural context (that of the 1980s), where collective projects and movements are declining. In other words, these issues can no longer be inserted into the context of socio-political movements fighting for socio-political transformation. In this new cultural environment of atomized individuals, different forms of socio-political transformation become important, namely individual learning on the one hand, and technocratic management on the other. Both are linked, and can perfectly be applied in today's cultural context in response to the new global issues; those are issues to which the individual person no longer has any immediate personal relation, and about which he or she can no longer be concerned in the traditional political way.

But will the media be sufficient to rouse the citizen's concern and moreover to mobilize him/her to action? Is concern and mobilization desirable in the perspective of global management? And what concrete role do the media play in this mobilization?

3.1 Transformation through media learning?

Every ecologically concerned person should but be pleased by the sudden attention given to such global issues as climate change, greenhouse effect, stratospheric ozone depletion, tropical rainforest destruction, etc., by the media and by some politicans, as well as by some prominent scientists. It can reasonably be argued that through such campaigns the general 'ecological awareness' of the public is increased. But will this awareness also lead to action, rather than to cynicism and despair? Should it actually lead to action?

Of course, there still exist inhabitants of the planet Earth who are living directly from or in close contact with nature. They of course do themselves increasingly begin to experience climatic anomalies like warming, drought and flood. In the Sahel, for example, drought and subsequent desertification has been under way for years. But only when these anomalies become more spectacular, as in the case of hurricanes, and start substantially to affect national economies—as did the drought in the US Midwest in 1987 and 1988—do they get media attention. If the desertification of the Sahel continued to be explained away by local causes such as ecological mismanagement, false development policies and of course overpopulation, the drought in the USA is now being explained in terms of global causes like climatic change, which is said to require global management.

The media play a key role in promulgating this explanation; but at the same time they also promote a general awareness of the new global isues: at the beginning of 1988 the 'Endangered Earth' was selected 'Planet of the year' by *Time* magazine. *National Geographic* had already asked one month before: 'Can man save this fragile Earth?'. Other journals followed up: 'The world is dying' (*Sunday Times*), 'SOS-Erde' (*Stern*), 'La Terre en danger de mort' (*L'Evènement du jeudi*), 'Menaces sur la Terre' (*L'Express*), 'Sauver la planète' (*Sciences et Avenir*), 'Wer rettet die Erde?' (*Der Spiegel*), 'Managing planet Earth' (*Scientific American*), etc., etc. And this is only a small part of the picture, since I should also mention the conspicuously growing international conference activity dealing with these global issues, and especially the media events covering these conferences.

But what exactly are the roles and the functions of the media in promoting these new global issues? It seems that one can distinguish between an optimistic and a pessimistic interpretation. The optimistic interpretation can consider the media coverage as a necessary step in rousing citizens' awareness, which in turn is considered a necessary condition for them to change their (individual) behavior. In this sense, the recent media coverage of the new global issues heralds in fact a new mode of environmental learning, i.e. a way which is probably adequate to the new type of global issues raised.

The pessimistic interpretation, on the other hand, can consider the media coverage as a first step in the creation among the citizenry of a general climate of acceptance of (coercive) management measures, which are presented as being inevitable. Both interpretations are possible, and the media may well fulfil both functions simultaneously.

3.2 Transformation through conferences and international treaties among global managers

Whenever the media inform the citizen about global environmental threats, they usually also describe the various global measures being taken in response to these threats. It is in this perspective that the media cover the increasing intergovernmental and expert conference activity, which usually result in treaties among nation-states, sometimes also including industry. Only in the field of stratospheric ozone depletion have there been three important intergovernmental conferences (Vienna, 1985; Montreal, 1987; Helsinki, 1989). Similar international meetings (with sometimes less concrete results) of experts have been held on climate change and global warming (Villach, 1985; Villach-Bellagio, 1987; Toronto, 1988), and there are many others to come.

The media generally give the picture that this kind of global management is not only capable of handling, but moreover is the only possible way to handle global environmental threats. I shall not deal here with the question whether or not this kind of global management will be effective. The point I want to raise here pertains to the kind of solution (to the global threats) the media presents to the citizen: it is always a kind of solution which asks (or forces) the citizen, in a top–down management approach, to change his individual behavior. This is in complete opposition to the 1970s: today, the citizen is considered the enemy, the real threat to the biosphere, whereas the political system knows and is the solution. In the 1970s the 'system' was the problem and the citizen the solution.

4. New global actors

The actors in this new trend are not movements, grassroots and local associations, nor simply concerned citizens. They are internationally organized scientists, particular research institutions and organizations, specific international agencies, as well as business-sponsored private institutes and national-states. Each of these actors has different interests. I will put the accent here on these actors, who, I think, are central to the promotion of this trend towards global environmental management. Scientific research institutions and organizations are in fact at its core, since they provide the kind of 'global' knowledge which allows other more policy-oriented institutions and agencies to translate it into practical 'global management strategies and policies'.

4.1 Scientific research institutions and international organizations

On the scientific level one finds mainly two actors promoting the new 'global' trend; one is US (scientific agency), the other international (scientific cooperation). The first has heavily influenced the second. Not should we forget the very important role of the USSR, where a similar evolution is taking place. I will not here consider developments in the USSR, because of the difficulty of access to the necessary information (e.g. Boudyko, 1980).

On the American side there is NASA, the National Aeronautics and Space Administration; already in 1982 NASA had launched, and in 1983 institutionalized at Columbia University, a global habitability program. In 1983, moreover, NASA appointed an Earth System Science Committee, which in 1988 produced an important report entitled: 'Earth system science. A program for global change'. This report makes concrete recommendations to NASA, NOAA (National Atmospheric and Oceanographic Administration) and NSF (US National Science Foundation), as well as to other US Federal Agencies.

The interest of the Earth system science program is at the same time scientific (modeling global change) and technological (monitoring global change, particularly from space). However, there is no doubt that US geo-political and military interests—which have shaped NASA since its beginnings (McDoughall, 1985)—are also part of the picture.

NASA is also closely linked to other American research institutions, which are equally important actors in this new global ecology trend. Among them must be mentioned UCAR (the University Corporation for Atmospheric Research), which, under the sponsorship of the National Science Foundation, operates the National Center for Atmospheric Research (NCAR), but also the Office for Interdisciplinary Earth Studies (OIES), both at Boulder, Colorado. In fact, Boulder has become something of a research center in the field of atmospheric science linked to global issues.

US research has been crucial in triggering off the other global ecological research program on an international level. This is the research project promoted by ICSU, the International Council of Scientific Unions, a federation of organizations of the natural sciences' various disciplines. At an international level, ISCU is a close partner of UNESCO and UNEP. This organization had already in 1969 created

SCOPE, the Scientific Committee on Problems of the Environment; SCOPE was particularly active in promoting the study of the big bio-geo-chemical cycles and the influence of human activity upon them.

In 1983, on the basis of an initiative by the US National Academy of Sciences, ICSU initiated and in 1986 formally launched IGBP, the *International Geosphere-Biosphere Program: A Study of Global Change* (NRC, 1983 & 1986; Malone and Roederer, 1985; IGBP, 1986, 1987 & 1988). The executive secretaryship of ICSU is today assumed by the Royal Swedish Academy of Sciences. The IGBP will rely heavily on space technologies and the kind of global information they produce. It will therefore depend on NASA, and other governments' national space agencies, as well as on specialized UN agencies like WMO and UNEP which are capable of producing the necessary information and financing corresponding research. This means that IGBP and Earth system science, like big science in general, will not be a politically, financially and technologically independent research enterprise.

This heavy dependence on (funding) agencies may explain why IIASA, the International Institute for Applied Systems Analysis, created in 1972 in Laxenburg (Austria) and once regarded as a promising new actor in the field of global ecology, has now lost ground. In fact, IIASA had in 1984, under its American director William Clark, launched the ambitious project for an interdisciplinary research program called 'Sustainable development of the biosphere' (Clark and Munn, 1986).

The underlying basic concepts and scientific conceptions of all these research institutions and organizations are very similar: planet Earth is seen as a system, say as a complex cybernetic 'machine'. This underlying conception is probably inherent to the epistemology of modern (technological) science, which means that whoever approaches global ecological issues in this dominantly scientific manner will end up considering planet Earth as a complex cybernetic machine, whose dysfunction requires global management.

4.2 Other, more policy-oriented actors in the new trend

A second type of actor is located in the political arena; more actively than the above-mentioned scientific research institutions and organizations, these actors try concretely to apply and put into practice knowledge of global ecological issues. What therefore characterizes all of them is the desire to link science to policy.

One of these actors is the United Nations system, within which some agencies play a specific role in the field of global ecology and global environmental management. UNESCO, which organized the first Conference on the Biosphere in 1968, had by 1971 launched the Man and Biosphere (MAB) program which embraces the main ecologically oriented activities of UNESCO (di Castri, 1981 & 1985). Research under the MAB is designed to provide the information necessary to solve practical problems of conservation and of the management of 'biosphere reserves' in various countries. However, only some MAB projects actually dealt with global ecological issues.

WMO, the World Meteorological Organization, is increasingly concerned with long-term climatic variations, especially since it first organized the World Climate Conference in Geneva in 1979. This conference gave birth to the World Climate Program (WMO, 1987), whose aim is to improve knowledge on climate variations and to assist decision-makers in planning and managing climate-sensitive activities. A second World Climate Conference was held in Geneva in 1990.

It is, however, UNEP, the United Nations Environment Program, based in Nairobi (Kenya) and created in 1972 by the Human Environment Conference in Stockholm, which is becoming increasingly prominent in this new trend toward global ecology (Tolba and White, 1979). UNEP's two main activities are in surveying and monitoring the global ecological situation and in environmental management. On the survey level, UNEP has established a permanent world survey system of the environment, called GEMS, the Global Environment Monitoring System; whereas GRID, the Global Resource Information Database, assesses world resources. The aim of such surveys is to understand cause–effect relations that should be taken into account in environmental management (UNEP, 1987). On the level of environmental management, one must mention UNEP's efforts to promote conventions intended to conciliate development projects with environmental considerations. I have already mentioned UNEP's efforts to protect the ozone layer (1985: the Vienna Convention; 1987: Montreal Protocole; 1989: Helsinki Declaration). Similar global management efforts are being made by UNEP in the field of tropical rainforest protection, in toxic waste management, as well as in wildlife conservation.

One further type of policy-related global actors is specialized institutes like the World Watch Institute, the multinational-sponsored International Environment Bureau, which has recently organized in Washington (May 1989) an important symposium on 'Global climate change', or the World Resources Institute. These institutes pursue research and environmental management along the same philosophical and epistemological line as IGBP or Earth System Science, but in a much more policy-oriented way, since they function as advisors and consultants to industry, to national governments and to international agencies.

The World Resources Institute (WRI), founded in 1982, is certainly the most typical body of this kind. Financed by private and corporate foundations, it focuses on policies and solutions to problems like the destruction of the tropical rain-forest, greenhouse effects like ozone depletion, and more generally on all kinds of global (economic) resource problems. Together with the International Institute for Environment and Development, another private and corporate-sponsored organization created in 1971, the WRI has since 1986 published an annual Report on World Resources.

All these more policy-related actors have a common socio-economic goal, called today 'sustainable development'. This nowadays famous concept is being promoted by the World Commission on Environment and Development, reporting on 'Our common future' (1987). Together with the scientific institutions and organizations the more policy-oriented actors share the concern as to how ecologically sustainable development can be achieved and maintained.

As equally important actors in this field of more policy-oriented activities in global ecology and global environmental management, one should also mention certain key journals which play a central role in international communication among globally ecologically minded persons: for example, *Ambio*, *The Ecologist*, *Environment*, and *Environmental Conservation*.

As we have seen in this chapter, a distinction can be made between scientific actors and more policy-oriented actors, which is in fact the distinction between global ecology and global environmental management. But both types of actors actually talk about the same new global ecological/environmental issues and imagine similar solutions to problems identified (i.e. mainly individual learning and global management). Nevertheless, there exist substantial differences in their ways of looking at global change.

5. Global ecology and global environmental management: what are they all about?

This chapter presents the two main new trends in the field of ecology, i.e. global ecology and global environmental management. These trends, promoted by experts and known up to now only to some specialists, should to my mind be presented in a way which makes them understandable to the wider public. This chapter is in itself based on an article written for a larger readership (Malone, 1986).

5.1 Global ecology

Global ecology is a scientific research trend which can be observed in some fields of the natural science community (atmospheric science, oceanographics, soil science, and similar fields). I do not want to explain this trend here, nor to trace back the evolution of its underlying conception of the biosphere. Suffice it to state that there actually do coexist two different versions or definitions of global ecology. They pertain to the two different disciplinary origins of this field: on the one hand there is a broad definition of global ecology, which looks at Earth in terms of comparative planetology. This definition expresses the interest of geophysiology, which seeks to understand the stability and the relative equilibrium of the Earth system. On the other hand, there is a more restrictive definition of global ecology, which goes back to the interests of the biologists, who are mainly concerned with the habitability of the Earth system. The term 'global ecology' allows us to link both definitions. Practical research activities will show whether the two sciences can collaborate.

Nevertheless, both definitions see planet Earth as a single complex system: 'A conceptual framework is emerging in which it is recognized that the terrestrial environment and the diverse forms of life that inhabit it constitute an integral system of intersecting components' (Malone, 1986, p. 6).

The main actors in this line of research are the US National Research Council (NRC), the US National Aeronautics and Space Administration (NASA), the US National Science Foundation (NSF), the International Council of Scientific Unions (ICSU), UNESCO, as well as the International Institute for Applied Systems Analysis (IIASA).

Global ecology is above all a project; this project aims at interdisciplinarity among the natural sciences, in particular at an integration of geophysics and global biology, of the physical sciences and the life sciences, as well as at 'breaking down the barriers that have traditionally compartmentalized the study of the atmosphere, the oceans, the solid part of the Earth, solar-terrestrial interaction, fauna and flora and humankind' (Malone, 1986, p. 8). Actually, however, there do exist in the field of global ecology different research projects: one is international, the others are American. The American projects have been the trigger for global ecological research.

The *International Geosphere-Biosphere Program: A Study in Global Change* (IGBP) had actually started in 1983, when ICSU declared that 'a central intellectual challenge of the next few decades is to deepen and strengthen our understanding of the interactions among the several parts of the geosphere and the biosphere' (Malone, 1986, p. 7). In September 1986 the IGBP was accepted by the 25th General Assembly of ICSU in Berne. IGBP started formally in 1986 and should continue at least up to the year 2000:

It will start with a preparatory build-up phase, during which pilot experiments will be designed and implemented, and then evolve to an operational phase in the early 1990s. Global monitoring will continue well into the next century. (Malone, 1986, p. 39)

The history of the IGBP goes back to ICSU's International Geophysical Year (IGY) in 1957/8, itself conceived as a successor to the International Polar Years (1882/3 and 1932/3). 'The first cooperative attempt by tens of thousands of scientists and technicians from 70 nations to gather information about the nature of the world, IGY marked the beginning of a new era in the science of the human habitat' (Malone, 1986, p. 8). It is interesting to note that IGY goes together with the beginning of the space age. IGY had two daughter programs, i.e. the International Biological Program (IBP) (1964–74) and the World Climate Research Program (WCRP) (since 1979). Nevertheless, ICSU has yet other global research programs under way: thus the World Ocean Circulation Experiment (WOCE), the Tropical Oceans and Global Atmosphere Program (TOGA), the International Solar Terrestrial Program (ISTP), not to mention, since 1969, SCOPE, the Scientific Committee on the Problem of the Environment. The existence of all these programs explain the synergy at the beginning of the 1980s leading to the IGBP.

The aim of the IGBP is (Malone, 1986, p. 8):

To describe and understand the interactive, physical, chemical and biological processes that regulate the total Earth system, the unique environment it provides for life, the changes that are occurring in that system, and the manner by which these changes are influenced by human actions.

Earth System Science is a NASA project which goes back to 1982 and its global Habitability Program:

The goal of Earth system science is to obtain a scientific understanding of the entire Earth system on a global scale by describing how its component parts and their interactions have evolved, how they function and how they may be expected to continue to evolve on all time scales. The challenge to Earth system science is to develop the capability to predict those changes that will occur in the next decade to century both naturally and in response to human activity (*Earth System Science*, 1988, p. 1).

Earth system science will involve three components:

1. An Earth Observing System (EOS), mainly based on satellites.

2. An advanced data system for data processing, data analysis and global modeling.
3. An interdisciplinary program of basic research that will ensure scientifically meaningful design for EOS. Programs specified are land-surface climatology, biomeatmospheric interaction, ocean circulation and biogeochemistry (Malone, 1986, p. 40).

This means that Earth system science in NASA is oriented less towards basic research and more toward the production of data. However, one must bear in mind that within the USA another part of the basic research in this field is also sponsored by the National Science Foundation, which is the equivalent of a National Academy of Sciences.

There are several reasons for the emergence of global ecology research: the first is internal to the scientific community and its dynamics as shown above. In this respect, one must note that global ecology actually offers a totally new field for the development of scientific research, namely a field with a perspective scientists and the public can (again) believe in.

A second reason is linked to the space age: 'the emerging capabilities of remote sensing from satellites are making possible global, synoptic measurements of life-sustaining, physical, chemical and biological processes' (Malone, 1986, p. 9). A third reason is linked to similar progress in mathematical modeling of global processes; and a fourth has probably to do with theoretical development in conceptualizing Earth and its biosphere.

The most important reason, however, is surely the anthropogenic changes and threats being exerted on the biosphere, though this is never explicitly stated. It is from these threats that global ecology draws its social legitimation. Within the scientific community two events in particular have created concern and a search for alternatives: one is the measurable destruction of the ozone layer since the 1960s; the other is the so-called 'nuclear winter' theory.

If the discovery of the ozone hole goes back to the late 1960s, perception of the environmental threats due to an even limited nuclear war goes back to SCOPE, the ICSU's Scientific Committee on the Problems of the Environment. It was SCOPE which launched, in 1982, a special study on the Environmental Consequences of Nuclear War (ENUWAR) (Crutzen, 1985). The corresponding report was published in 1985 (SCOPE, 1985), offering to the scientific community for the first time mathematical proof that Man, through nuclear war, is capable of destroying the biosphere (i.e. the theory of 'nuclear winter', e.g. Ehrlich et al., 1984). One can consider with Virilio (1983) that

nuclear war is just an accelerated version of a more general war Man
conducts against the biosphere.

This scientific proof has anthropological (cultural) implications
which reach far beyond the scientific community, and goes together
with another awareness, produced by the same trend and of similar
anthropological significance. In fact, space technology has for the first
time in the history of humankind offered the possibility of looking at
planet Earth from space and observing its uniqueness and delicacy:

The era of planetary exploration during the 1970s and 1980s resulted in a
treasure trove of knowledge about nearly all the planets known to the
ancients. We came to realize how unique, exquisite, and interesting is Earth
among the planets of the solar system. Its physical, chemical, and biological
evolution over billions of years produced an environment benign for living
creatures. Earth is the most interesting planet in the solar system and one
worthy of intensive study (Malone, 1986, p. 8).

With modern planetary exploration has come a sense of the uniqueness and
delicate position of the ecological niche occupied by the Earth in the solar
system. As a result, we now recognize that the limits of a living biosphere are
so narrow that even very small variations in the flow of life supporting energy
from the sun could spell the difference between benign and hostile environment (Friedman, 1985, p. 44).

But this anthropologically and epistemologically totally new contribution of global ecology will remain without consequences if this
uniqueness of planet Earth and our capacity to destroy it are not
understood by its inhabitants in a way that will change their behavior.

Further developments are based on perception of this uniqueness
and on a theoretical understanding of the role of life and man in the
evolution of planet Earth. Grinevald (1987a) has traced back this
conception by establishing a theoretical and intellectual link between
global ecology (Earth system), Vernadsky's idea of the 'biosphere' and
Lovelock's Gaia hypothesis.

The core concept in this new trend toward global ecology is the
'Earth system'. Epistemologically this is a complex mixture between a
mechanical and organistic approach. Man, as an observer, a researcher
and a manager is not considered part of this system. He places himself
outside of it, probably somewhere in a satellite, looking at the Earth
system as if it were but another spaceship. Global ecology (IGBP,
Earth system science) is mostly interested in the way the Earth system
functions, no matter how complex this 'machinery' ultimately is. As a
global manager, Man's aim is to keep this system functioning; some
even think its functioning can and should be improved.

In the idea of a biosphere life becomes an active part of the Earth system; Friedman (1985, p. 20) defines it as follows: 'The Biosphere is the integrated living and life-supporting system comprising the peripheral envelope of Planet Earth together with its surrounding atmosphere so far down, and up, as any form of life exists naturally.'

In fact, this definition goes back to the proposal for an 'International year of the biosphere' by the journal *Environmental Conservation*. There is nevertheless debate as to the role life actually plays in the Earth system; is it an active, regulatory role, as James Lovelock thinks (1979 & 1988), or a more passive adaptatory one in the sense of geophysics? In any case, life can be integrated in the functioning of the Earth system without changing the underlying, more or less mechanistic conception.

The Gaia hypothesis (Lovelock, 1979 & 1988) not only accepts the active role of life in maintaining the homeostasis of the biosphere, but moreover states that the biosphere has been created by life; therefore, the biosphere in itself can be considered as a 'living organism'. Further, Gaia is not only a hypothesis about the active role of life in maintaining the homeostasis of the geophysiological Earth system, it is also a theory of the role of man and his conscience, as well as of his responsibility for Gaia: if Lovelock, a former consultant to NASA, speaks of 'Earth as a living organism', he in fact means a living, highly complex, self-organizing system. Man, science and technology are, according to him, inextricably involved in this evolutionary process toward increased complexity and self-organization. At a certain stage in the process, planetary consciousness is said to emerge; this consciousness is incarnated by man and made possible by (space) technology, another element in the same evolutionary process. In this perspective, Man, the incarnation of global consciousness, naturally ends up being responsible for the Earth system and its management.

In this evolutionary approach the Gaia hypothesis actually adds a teleological, but also a spiritual dimension to Earth system science. A source for this philosophy is the notion of the 'noosphere' introduced in the 1920s by Teilhard de Chardin, le Roy and Vernadsky (Grinevald, 1987a). Lovelock, in this way, can argue how Man, and in particular some natural scientists, will become the future global managers. The Gaia hypothesis thus actually prepares the fusion of global ecology with another profound and important trend today; that is, the 'new age' movement, which considers individual and global consciousness as the solution to today's crisis. This 'new age' trend is a typical expression of an observable mythologization of Gaia (or Planet Earth), a phenomenon which has its roots not only in the increasing threats to Gaia, but also in the growing individualism, which leaves it up to each individual person to elaborate his relation to nature.

In conclusion, it must be stated that global ecology does not in itself lead to global environmental management. In fact, scientists are constantly pointing out how fragile their knowledge actually is, and that we are part of a global experiment whose outcome is unknown. Ravetz (1986) has theorized this and proposes that new criteria must be elaborated by science, which will allow decisions on the basis of 'ultimate scientific proof'; he suggests that at present politicans and managers need to learn how to make decisions on the basis of 'usable ignorance'.

Nevertheless there exist, in my opinion, two main reasons why global ecology will in any case lead to global environmental management; the first is that there are today no alternatives to growth and development; but if growth and development have to be pursued, global environmental management will certainly be the only possible solution. The second reason is that global change research ignores social, economic, political and above all cultural dimensions; in the absence of such considerations, management seems an easy and feasible thing to do.

5.2 Global environmental monitoring and management

Global environmental monitoring and management aim at putting into political and economic practice the most relevant knowledge produced by global ecology and allied research.

It is evident that global environmental management more or less directly results from global ecology research; this is even implicitly stated as a goal of IGBP:

The IGBP will be a carefully designed programme of research directed at providing the information we need to assess the future of the Earth in the next 100 years, with an emphasis on processes that change on time scales of decades to centuries. It will be a programme of basic research with almost immediate practical applications in the management of resources at national and international levels and as a means of improving the reliability of warnings of global change of significance to our environment and to humankind (IGBP, 1986, p. 1).

Global environmental management therefore has to do with first, anticipating global change in order that adequate measures can be taken in reaction to this change, as well as with second, assessing the state and the evolution of (living) resources. This idea was in fact already present in the *World Strategy for Conservation* (IUCN/UNEP/ WWF, 1980), which spoke of 'resource management'. Be it resources or pollution, they can now be identified, measured and monitored, mainly from space.

In this sense, global environmental management is also a direct result of the technology used by global ecological research, i.e. mainly environmental monitoring by satellites, called 'remote sensing'. Knowledge produced in such a way can of course also be used for other than research purposes:

The profound implications [of global ecology, MF] for the management of the [se] resources are already looming. It is now within our reach to take the processes in biomes and link them quantitatively to global models characterizing the behavior of the atmosphere and the oceans (Malone, 1986, p. 8).

In this way, global managers—who can be multinationals, national governments or international agencies—can dispose of a type of knowledge which enables them to plan investments, to anticipate economic (and therefore socio-political) problems, and, for the superpowers, to develop or reconsider (new) geo-political strategies. Concrete 'policies' pertaining, for example, to soil management, to land management, to water management, etc., translate management strategies into political action.

The idea of global management is, at least partially, the result of a global urgency. But it is also the result of scientific and technological possibilities which today allow economy and politics to think on such a global scale. In order to remain competitive on the market, multinationals today actually need to anticipate global change (drought, warming, flood, etc.), as well as to anticipate the evolution of (living) resources. In order to avoid political problems (riots, upheavals, etc.) national governments need to foresee global change and to evaluate its major effects. In order to place themselves in a geo-politically favorable position, the superpowers have a vital interest in anticipating possible global change.

One can argue that such use of global ecology and global environmental management is a perversion or an exploitation of a scientific and technological activity which is fundamentally good, or neutral. But one can also argue that at least some sort of technocratic management is rooted in the very nature of recent global isues and knowledge of them; as for example in the case of the ozone hole, knowledge can only be produced by a few experts relying on sophisticated technological equipment. It is a type of knowledge which has hardly any local significance or at least cannot be measured on a local level by the concerned citizen. It is therefore a type of knowledge which, in its very nature, is meant either for global managers or to be spread by the media, or both.

Assuming that global ecological knowledge is not perverted or exploited for business or strategic purposes, can in this case global environmental management be a solution to the problems identified? At the present moment, one can only speculate; I personally have my doubts. In any case, global environmental management—even if conceived in a positive perspective of saving humanity through sustainable development—will have its price, which is global technocracy, i.e. more or less the end of democracy.

Even William Clark, who has probably furthest explored possible political, and not only technocratic responses to global change, concludes with 'political' management strategies (energy management, land management, ocean management) on the level of the nation-states and/or on an international level (among nation-states) (Clark, 1989). Global environmental management will lead to an increase in technocratic (state) power, accompanied by a discourse, or rather a 'gospel of global efficiency' (Sachs, 1988). Only 'more power' and 'more management' will, in this global management perspective, be an adequate answer to global change. It is therefore highly likely that global environmental management will re-enforce existing power structures, above all the nation-state, as well as give birth to new, probably more international ones.

Nevertheless, global environmental management is built on two implicit assumptions, both of which can be questioned: the first says that the pursuit of (industrial) development, even if sustainable, is desirable, necessary or inevitable. And in fact all the new global actors draw at least part of their legitimation from this implicit assumption. Another part of their legitimation is derived from the assumption that global management will be an adequate answer to global change.

Both assumptions are in total opposition to the ecological movements' ideology of the 1970s: at that time, development in this form was heavily criticized, and technocracy seemed unacceptable. This is another proof that we are dealing here with a totally new trend in the field of ecology, characterized by new issues, promoted by new actors and based on new philosophical concepts and conceptions. It is still unclear to me what will become of the traditional actors in the field of ecology (mainly ecological movements, but also green parties) as this trend gains ground.

Moreover, it is my conviction that global environmental management will fail, since I cannot imagine that some global managers can do better in half a century than nature in 3.5 billion years. It should also be stated that global environmental management is no alternative to the present crisis: global environmental management simply continues the 'civilization of power'. Although presented as a simple instrument, global environmental management is in permanent danger of becoming a goal in itself, since it does not say anything about goals, or about content.

6. Critics of global ecology and global environmental management

Apart from the above-mentioned criticism, global ecology and global environmental management contain one major weakness from which several other defects can be deduced: they consider the Earth system as an entity which is independent of society. I will show here that society has not really been analyzed as a possible cause of global change. Therefore global environmental management will not get at the very roots of global change.

6.1 Comment 1: undifferentiated analysis of anthropogenic effects

Be it the concept of the 'Earth system', the 'Biosphere' or the more spiritual concept of 'Gaia', in any case considerations of the causes of global change are eliminated and replaced by measurements of effects like, for example, the increase in CO_2. The sources of these effects are attributed to 'Man', to 'humanity', to the 'human race', to 'humankind', at most to 'human society', but never to economic or industrial development, not to speak of a more sophisticated analysis of the causes. The following quotation is typical of this fuzzy way of talking about the cause of global change:

> The human race now exerts a major influence on the chemistry of the atmosphere and on the allocation of resources on land, and is increasingly an influence on the ocean. As human society controls and modifies the environment, both deliberately and involuntarily, these changes begin to exert a feedback effect on the development of society—another nonlinear interaction, now with intervention of the newest component of the biosphere, the Anthroposphere (Roederer, 1985, p. 10).

But can one still speak of 'effects' when 'the human impacts on the Earth now approximate the scale of the natural, interactive processes that control the global life support system' (ICSU, 1986, p. 2)?

In fact, there is no sound analysis of the causes: global ecology and global environmental management do not seek to analyze or to understand the anthropogenic origins. What is instead sought is how the underlying Earth system reacts and functions, how global change evolves and how it can be managed. In particular, there are no considerations pertaining to the role of politics, of economy, of psychology, of culture, etc., which shape the relation of societies with their natural environment. Necessarily, the only imaginable solutions to today's ecological/environmental problems are seen in a-political and a-cultural global, technocratic management.

6.2 *Comment 2: naive conception of politics*

Since there is no differentiated analysis of the causes of global change, there is also no sophisticated conception in response to it: all responses take the form of (global) management. For the global manager, politics is a simple tool, which takes the form of national and international policies. Energy policies, for example, will reduce CO^2 emissions, and/or—and this is the belief of many global managers—further the development of nuclear power as a response to global warming.

This highly naive conception of (political) management through the nation-state using, I assume, its monopoly of power and organized violence, first, does not consider any other forms of socio-political transformation than coercive (state) measures, and second, totally disregards the citizen, regardless of the fact that his behavior must be at the roots of any kind of transformation. In other words, there is no idea how to translate global management strategies concretely into learning and local actions, in particular into actions which will receive the active support of the citizen. Says Caldwell (1985, p. 195–6), a specialist in the relations between politics and ecology since the beginning of the 1970s:

What is needed, but is not present, is a popular movement, fundamentally political, to translate the oughts and shoulds of environmental findings and declarations into workable and widely acceptable programs and action. Information and education alone will not move people and their governments. Means must be found for translating our growing knowledge of requirements for a sustainable future into widespread popular belief in the desirability and the possibility of such a future. Conceptual obstacles to such belief must be identified and so far as possible neutralized and removed. Unless the root causes of environmental decay are overcome, the Biosphere will not be saved.

Both criticisms—the undifferentiated analysis of the causes and the naive conception of politics—should in fact not be addressed to global ecology or global environmental management, but to the social sciences. Instead, one could criticize global ecology and global environmental management for not having taken into account the relevant expertise of the social sciences—if there was any.

7. Conclusion toward a possible role of peace research

Throughout this chapter I have highlighted several weaknesses in global change research and global environmental management; they all have to do with the fact that society is not adequately taken into account. It seems to me important to identify these weaknesses clearly, since my recommendations will be developed as a constructive response to them.

The prime weakness of global change research is the status it attributes to Man: in fact, global ecology does not consider Man; it simply measures his anthropogenic effects on the biosphere. Global environmental management, again, operates with an image of Man as a mass individual, who is a problem and in no way a possible partner. The social sciences, finally, certainly care about Man, but totally neglect Man's relation with and dependence on the biosphere. It is an urgent task to define an adequate status and role for Man in the biosphere. On the one hand, the biosphere (now) imposes limits upon Man, which will have to be encompassed by the social sciences. In this perspective the social sciences will probably have to undergo a profound transformation. On the other hand, Man has also to be included in global ecology, no longer as a simple effect, but as a 'bio-geo-chemical' factor, transforming the biosphere.

But here arises a second weakness, i.e. the very conception of Man: in fact, global ecology and global environmental management have a more than simplistic conception of Man as an a-cultural, a-political and a-social individual. It is this conception of Man which explains the undifferentiated analysis of anthropogenic effects, as well as the naive approach to politics. If one considers that today's global ecological crisis is not simply a technical problem, nor a purely political, social or economic one, but that it has cultural origins and dimensions, a cultural, human science approach is called for to understand the crisis. This means that eventual ways out of the crisis cannot be simply technological fixes, or isolated political, social and economic measures; these will have to be embedded in a (new) cultural framework. But, how can such a cultural framework be brought about? The social sciences have elaborated a considerable amount of knowledge as to how societies function independent of or even in opposition to the biosphere. Such knowledge is of course necessary; but this knowledge has to be incorporated in a more general understanding of the way cultures evolve in interaction with the biosphere. In such an understanding alone lies a hope for alternative relations to the biosphere.

This cultural approach also highlights a third weakness which global ecology and global environmental management share: namely the purely instrumental, i.e. highly uncritical conception of economic growth and of techno-scientific development. They might be instrumental in building up modern society and in finding solutions to some of its problems, but they are more than instrumental when it comes to shaping our culture, i.e. our societies' relations with the biosphere. If we consider that a cultural transformation is a necessary condition for a way out of today's global ecological crisis, these media which shape our relation with nature (i.e. economic growth and (scientific) technology) must also be affected by this transformation. They will therefore have to be looked upon as a problem, and no longer necessarily as a solution to the problem. The same remark can be applied to the nation-state, which is the ultimate legitimation of economic growth and techno-scientific development.

It seems to me that peace research has built up, over the years, considerable expertise in these fields. As we are increasingly shifting from the concept of 'national security' to a concept of 'common security', it becomes more and more important for peace researchers to know about global ecological issues, as well as the global environmental management strategies under way. I hope this text has provided this basic introductory knowledge. The next step could now be a critical analysis of the peace research field, evaluating its possible contribution to global change research.

Notes

1. The author would like to thank Jacques Grinevald for his assistance.

References

Barney, G. (ed.), 1980. *The Global 2000 Report to the President. Entering the Twenty-First Century*. Penguin: Harmondsworth.

Boudyko, M., 1980. *Ecologie globale*. Editions du Progrès: Moscow.

Brown, L. and Flavin, C., 1988. 'The Earth's vital signs', in L. Brown et al., *State of the World*. Norton: New York.

Caldwell, L., 1985. 'Science will not save the biosphere but politics might', *Environmental Conservation*, vol. 12, no. 3.

di Castri, F. et al., 1981. 'MAB: the Man and the Biosphere Program as an evolving system', *Ambio*, vol. X, nos. 2–3.

di Castri, F., 1985. 'Twenty years of international programmes on ecosystems and the biosphere: an overview of achievements, shortcomings and possible new perspectives', in T.F. Malone and J.G. Roederer (eds), *Global Change*. Cambridge University Press: New York.

Clark, W., 1989. 'Für eine neue Qualität politischer und wirtschaftlicher

Zusammenarbeit', in P. Crutzen and M. Müller (eds), *Das Ende des blauen Planeten? Der Klimakollaps: Gefahren und Auswege*. Beck: München.

Clark, W. and Holling, C., 1985. 'Sustainable development of the biosphere: human activities and global change', in T.F. Malone and J.G. Roederer (eds), *Global Change*. Cambridge University Press: New York.

Clark, W. and Munn, R.E., (eds), 1986. *Sustainable Development of the Biosphere*. Cambridge University Press: Cambridge.

Crutzen, P., 1985. 'The global environment after nuclear war', *Environment*, vol. 27, no. 8.

Earth System Science. A Program for Global Change, 1988. NASA: Washington DC.

Ehrlich, P. et al., 1984. *The Cold and the Dark. The World After Nuclear War*. Norton: New York.

Friedman, H., 1985. 'The science of global change—an overview', in T.F. Malone and J.G. Roederer (eds), *Global Change*. Cambridge University Press: New York.

Grinevald, J., 1984. *Le développement de la crise planétaire et le catastrophisme de l'âge nucléaire. Repérages Bibliographiques*, no. 26. Institut Universitaires d'Études du Développement: Genève.

Grinevald, J., 1987a. 'Le développement de/dans la biosphère', in *L'Homme inachevé. Cahiers de l'IUED*. PUF: Paris.

Grinevald, J., 1987b. 'On a holistic concept for deep and global ecology: the biosphere', *Fundamenta Scientiae*, vol. 8, no. 2.

ICSU/Ad Hoc Planning Group on Global Change, 1986. *The International Geosphere–Biosphere Programme: A Study of Global Change*. Report prepared for the 21st General Assembly, Berne, September 14–19, 1986, 4 pages.

IGBP, 1986. *Global Change*, report no. 1.

IGBP, 1987. *Global Change*, report no. 2.

IGBP, 1988. *Global Change*, reports nos. 3 and 4.

IUCN/UNEP/WWF, 1980. *World Strategy for Conservation. The Conservation of Living Resources in the Service of a Sustainable Development*. IUCN: Gland.

Lovelock, J., 1979. *Gaia. A New Look at Life on Earth*. Oxford University Press: New York.

Lovelock, J., 1988. *The Ages of Gaia. A Biography of Our Living Earth*. Oxford University Press: New York.

Malone, T.F., 1986. 'Mission to planet Earth. Integrating studies of global change', *Environment*, vol. 28, no. 8.

Malone, T.F. and Roederer, J.G. (eds), 1985. *Global Change*. Cambridge University Press: New York.

McDoughall, W., 1985. *The Heavens and the Earth. A Political History of the Space Age*. Basic Books: New York.

Meadows, D. et al., 1972. *The Limits to Growth. A Report for the Club of Rome's Project on the Predicament of Mankind*. Universe Books: New York.

National Research Council, 1983. *Toward an International Geosphere-*

30   *Mathias Finger*

Biosphere Program. A Study of Global Change. National Academy Press: Washington DC.

National Research Council, 1986. *Global Change in the Geosphere-Biosphere. Initial Priorities for an IGBP.* National Academy Press: Washington DC.

Ravetz, J., 1986. 'Usable knowledge, usable ignorance: incomplete science with policy implications', in W. Clark and R.E. Munn (eds), *Sustainable Development of the Biosphere.* Cambridge University Press: London.

Roederer, J.R., 1985. 'The proposed International Geosphere-Biosphere Program: some special requirements for disciplinary coverage and program design', in T.F. Malone and J.G. Roederer (eds), *Global Change.* Cambridge University Press: New York.

Sachs, W., 1988. 'The gospel of global efficiency', *IFDA Dossier*, no. 68.

SCOPE, 1985. *Environmental Consequences of Nuclear War*, SCOPE report, no. 28. John Wiley: New York.

Tolba, M. and White, G., 1979. 'Global life support systems. A joint statement', *UNEP Information*, vol. 47.

UNEP, 1987. *Environmental Data Report.* Basil Blackwell: London.

Virilio, P., 1983. *Pure War.* Foreign Agent Series: New York.

WMO, 1987. *The Global Climate System. Autumn 1984–Spring 1986.* WMO: Geneva.

World Commission on Environment and Development, 1987. *Our Common Future.* Oxford University Press: New York.

3 Conflict in the Use and Management of International Commons

Marvin S. Soroos

1. Introduction

This chapter explores the types of conflict that typically arise in the use and the management of resource domains traditionally treated as international commons. The most notable of these international commons are the oceans, fisheries, the seabed, Antarctica, outer space (including the geostationary orbit), the atmosphere, the electromagnetic spectrum (better known as the airwaves), and aquifers that span international boundaries.[1] The concept *commons*, as popularized in Garrett Hardin's (1968) often quoted essay 'The tragedy of the commons', refers to a resource domain that is subject to a particular type of legal arrangement, known as *res communis*, in which a designated group of actors are permitted to make simultaneous use of a resource domain for their private benefit. Under the rules of the commons, individual operators may take possession of what is produced from a resource domain, for example the grass consumed by their cattle on the common pasture in Hardin's mythical village, or the specific fish they catch in their nets. However, individuals have no legal right to stake a permanent exclusive claim to all or part of the resource domain, namely the pasture or the entire fishery in the examples. An *international commons* is a resource domain that is shared by more than one state; ones that are shared by all states may be referred to as a *global commons*.

A resource domain ceases to be a commons when the rules of usage change so that individual members of the community are no longer permitted to exploit the whole domain for their private gain. For example, a domain that is subdivided, with sections assigned to individual members of the community for their exclusive use, ceases to be a commons. However, rules on the *amount* of usage of a resource domain, such as the quantity of pollutants that may be emitted into the atmosphere, are not inconsistent with a commons arrangement. The existence of such rules implies a regulated commons.

While a resource domain that is handled as a commons may also have the attributes of a *common property resource*, the two concepts should not be used interchangeably. Whereas a commons is defined in terms of the legal provisions for use of a resource domain, common property resources are distinguished by their physical attributes. A common property resource is one that can be subjected to joint use, meaning not only that several users can derive benefits from using the resource, but also that overuse or misuse can diminish the resource's value to all users. In addition, such a resource domain cannot be feasibly divided into private sections, nor is it practicable to exclude unauthorized users (Oakerson, 1986, pp. 15–19; Wijkman, 1982, p. 515). The atmosphere, which circulates unhindered over the boundaries of political jurisdictions, is a good illustration of a resource domain that has the physical attributes of a common property resource and the legal status of an international commons.

2. Conflicts arising from incompatible uses of international commons

An unregulated commons is a fertile ground for conflicts of interest among users. The potential for conflict over international commons has increased greatly as a result of the much heavier demands being placed on them due to population growth, industrialization, and technological changes. Conflicts typically arise when one state's use of the resource domain is incompatible with the interests of another country.

Several types of interest incompatibility are possible. First, a situation of *mutually exclusive consumption* arises when the harvesting of a resource by one state precludes its consumption by another. Thus, the same fish caught by one country cannot be caught by another; nor can any given nodule on the seabed be mined by more than one country. Mutually exclusive consumption is not grounds for a serious conflict of interest when the resource is plentiful enough to allow the operators from all countries to achieve the level of consumption they desire. This was largely the case with the bounty of the oceans' living resources until recent decades, when worldwide harvesting of fish sharply intensified, seriously depleting fisheries.

A second form of incompatibility occurs when there is *interference between similar uses* of a resource domain. An example is the various frequencies, or wavelengths, that comprise the electromagnetic spectrum. Unless simultaneous transmitters of radio waves on the same frequencies are sufficiently distant, the signals of two or more broadcasters will intermingle. The result is static for receivers of the signals, which diminishes the usefulness of that segment of the spectrum. The potential for interference between transmissions to and from satellites is a factor limiting the overall capacity of the geostationary orbit for satellite communications.

Incompatibility is also present when there is *interference between dissimilar uses* of a commons. In Hardin's English village, such a situation would arise if certain members of the community desired to cultivate the pasture area for growing vegetables whereas others wanted to continue using it for grazing cattle. Those who would use the oceans as a dump for their wastes, including highly toxic substances, may interfere with fishing interests whose catches may become worthless if contaminated with these pollutants.

Conflicts of interest are present when one use of a commons causes *collateral damage* to the territory or property of other actors. Atmospheric pollutants are a good illustration of this. Acid precipitation resulting from emissions of air pollutants destroys forests and freshwater aquatic life and damages buildings and metal structures far from the source of the pollutants. Discharges of oil from grounded tankers that foul the shorelines of nearby coastal states are another form of collateral damage, as are the hazards from the debris of disabled satellites that occasionally plunge to the earth's surface.

Finally, some uses of commons by one state jeopardize the security of other states. The oceans have been used for many centuries as a medium for launching attacks from military vessels, and during the twentieth century for the operations of submarines. Satellites in outer space are a means of military reconnaissance. The economic security of coastal fishing states may be undermined by intensive fishing by deep-sea fleets in nearby waters. The economic and environmental security of many states is jeopardized by the global warming phenomenon that is caused primarily by the buildup of carbon dioxide in the atmosphere due to human activities.

These types of conflict can be very costly for the users of international commons because of the diminished benefits that they derive from it. Costly investments in fishing fleets and satellite communications systems may prove to be unproductive. The overall costs resulting from the numerous types of damage caused by acid precipitation are incalculable, but certainly enormous, as will be the expense of adjusting to the environmental consequences of global warming. Of special interest to peace research are numerous historical instances in which tensions over conflicting uses have soured relations between states, occasionally escalating into armed confrontations and even full-blown wars. During the 1960s, the United Kingdom and Iceland, two allies that were unlikely combatants, became embroiled in a confrontation known as the 'Cod War' over fishing rights off the coast of Iceland. Similarly, the so-called 'Tuna War' occurred when Ecuador and Peru took steps to limit fishing by United States boats off the west coast of South America.

3 Strategies for managing incompatible uses of international commons

In this section we will consider several strategies of conflict resolution that can be employed to manage incompatible uses of joint resource domains, along with illustrations of how they have been applied to international commons in the form of multilateral treaties.

3.1 Bans on certain uses of a resource domain

Some uses of international commons may be deemed intolerable and thus prohibited entirely, or allowed only under certain circumstances. Resource domains subject to such a prohibition cease to be commons for that use, since they are no longer open for the benefit of the individual. Such is the case with the Limited Test-Ban Treaty (1963), which prohibits the testing of nuclear devices in the atmosphere, the waters of the oceans, and outer space. Other treaties prohibit the locating of nuclear weapons on the seabed, on Antarctic, and in outer space. The 1972 London Convention on ocean dumping 'blacklists' certain highly toxic types of waste that cannot be disposed of in the oceans under any circumstances, and established a 'gray list' of less toxic chemicals that can be dumped only under prescribed conditions after a special permit has been secured.

3.2 Limits on the amount of use of a resource domain

When the resources of a commons are not large enough to accommodate the demands placed upon it by its users, it may be necessary to ration the amount of use by each user. The herdsmen in Hardin's village may each be allowed a maximum number of cattle, with any additional ones being confiscated. Several of the international fishery commissions have enacted quotas specifying the amount of fish each country is allowed to harvest each year to keep the combined catch within the 'maximum sustainable yield'. Similarly, agreements have been reached on target reductions for air pollutants, most notably the 1985 Protocol to the Convention on Long-Range Transboundary Pollution (1979), which obliges ratifiers to reduce sulfur emissions 30% below 1980 levels by 1993, and the Montreal Protocol on depletion of the ozone layer (1987), which imposed an immediate freeze on the production of CFCs at 1986 levels and a 20% reduction by 1993 and 50% by 1998.

3.3 Rules on how a resource domain is used

Conflicts on how a commons is used can be managed not only by the extent but also by the *manner* of its use. Rules of the International Maritime Organization pertaining to the construction of supertankers, the navigational equipment on them, and the training of their crews, have reduced the incidence of pollution-causing accidents. International fishery commissions have adopted rules on the types of nets that can be used in order to preserve fisheries on which numerous countries depend. Specifications on the type of equipment used to send radio signals can greatly enhance the capacity of bands of the electromagnetic spectrum.

3.4 Exclusive concessions to parts of a resource domain

Some conflicts that arise under the commons arrangement can be managed by recognizing exclusive rights of individual actors for specified uses of assigned parts of a resource domain. The concession may be for a specific period and be subject to certain stipulations that are set internationally. Thus, the ultimate authority over the area is not transferred to the user but retained by the community as a whole. Such an arrangement is not possible for common property resources such as the atmosphere or highly migratory fisheries, because their physical properties rule out assignments of parts of the resource domain.

Such concessions are sometimes granted to the first established user of a part of a domain, what is known as the *first-come, first-served* rule, or pejoratively as 'squatter's rights'. Subsequent would-be users of the same sector are expected to avoid interfering with the recognized first user of that sector. This arrangement may be implemented by the creation of a registry of first users, which later would-be users would be obliged to check to certify that their new operations would not infringe on previously established users. Such an arrangement has been established for first users of electromagnetic frequencies and locations for satellites in the geostationary orbit, both through the International Frequencies Registration Board of the International Telecommunications Union.

Exclusive concessions can be awarded on the basis of other criteria. Market economists often argue for *auctioning* the concessions to the highest bidder on the presumption that those who plan to use the resource domain the most productively will be willing to pay the highest price. Alternatively, an a priori *allocation* can be made which reserves a segment of a resource domain for each member of the community for his exclusive use. Those who are not able to make immediate use of their reserved segments would then be entitled to lease them, presumably to the highest bidder. No examples come to mind of auctioning rights to an international resource domain, but an a priori allocation plan has been adopted for satellite 'parking places' in the geostationary orbit.

3.5 Partition of the resource domain

The division of a resource domain can be taken one step further, with full control over sections being permanently transferred to individual users. The transfer may imply assigning ownership or, at the international level, the assumption of sovereignty over the domain by specific states. Hardin is partial to a partitioning of the village pasture and other resource domains whenever possible because it makes the users more accountable for the consequences of overuse and misuse of them.

This is the principal strategy adopted in the new Law of the Sea Treaty for managing conflict over coastal fisheries. The band of territorial waters over which a coastal state can exercise virtually all of the prerogatives of sovereignty was expanded from 3 to 12 nautical miles from the shoreline. Coastal states will also have the first claim to the resources of the oceans in an 'exclusive economic zone' (EEZ) that extends 200 nautical miles from the shoreline. These zones encompass most of the world's productive fisheries. Further negotiations are needed on how to manage highly migratory species that move across the borders of EEZs.

3.6 Public monopoly

Transferring the rights to exploit a resource domain from individual operators to a community enterprise is a more radical strategy in managing conflicts arising under the commons arrangement. In the context of the English village, all of the grazing on the community pasture would be done by a publicly owned herd. The proceeds would be distributed equally among the members of the community or unequally on the basis of established criteria such as family size, financial need, or number of cattle originally donated to the public herd.

Public monopolies are of limited applicability in exploiting international resource domains. It is hard to imagine how all activities that emit pollutants into the atmosphere could be transferred to an international public corporation, or similarly all uses of the electromagnetic spectrum. All rights to fish the oceans or position satellites in geostationary orbit could conceivably be transferred as an international fishing enterprise, but it is very unlikely that states with established uses of these resources would accept such a scheme.

At the most recent United Nations Conference on the Law of the Sea (1973–82), Third World states argued that an international enterprise, set up as an arm of the International Seabed Authority, should be given a monopoly over mining of the seabed in areas beyond the jurisdiction of coastal states. In the end, a compromise was reached that provides for 'parallel' mining by an international enterprise and private companies.

4. Conflicts that arise over management strategies

The schemes for managing a resource domain that were outlined in the previous section have some potential for averting disruptive conflicts that arise among users under the commons arrangement. However, because these alternatives affect the various users of resource domains differently, they raise additional conflicts of interest which must be addressed before agreement can be reached on implementing them.

The most basic conflict arises between different degrees of commitment to addressing the problems that occur when the resource domain is handled as a commons. For example, some states such as the low-lying Maldive Islands, which are in danger of being submerged by rising sea levels, are much more dedicated to international action that would slow global warming than are others which may even benefit from a longer growing season.

At the next stage, which assumes agreement on the need for changes in the rules on the use of a resource domain, there may be fundamental disagreements on which of the basic approaches should be adopted and implemented. For example, coastal states have preferred the partitioning of ocean space in a way that gives them jurisdiction over areas off their coasts along the lines of the EEZs established in the new ocean treaty, in contrast to states with distant-water fleets whose interests would be better served by maintaining a commons but with rules that limit the catch.

Even if a consensus exists on what the basic approach should be, agreement may be very difficult to reach on specific provisions. For example, in setting national quotas for fish catches by international fishery commissions, conflicts have arisen over the relative weights that should be given to criteria such as geographic proximity to a fishery, the size of past harvests, and investments in fishing fleets. Should provisions be made for additional countries that apply for a share in the catch?

5. Typical lines of conflict between states

Certain conflicts between states arise repeatedly as strategies are devised for managing the use of international resource domains. The opposing positions normally reflect the diverse attributes of states or the situations with which they must cope, several of which are briefly described in this section.

5.1 Economic circumstances

The priorities of leaders are shaped in a significant way by the economic conditions of their states, not only their general level of development, but also short-term circumstances. In poorer states, investments in conserving the environment have often been looked upon as a luxury that can be indulged in by more prosperous countries not confronted by the harsh realities of widespread poverty and burdensome foreign debt. This type of thinking is becoming less prevalent with a growing worldwide awareness that economic development and the preservation of natural resources go hand in hand. Nevertheless, economic realities continue to limit severely the options available to most Third World countries.

For example, given its current economic predicament, Poland is not in a position to make a commitment to cut its own emissions by the percentages spelled out in recent treaties on transboundary pollution, even though as a heavy importer of pollutants from neighboring countries, Poland has a substantial stake in reciprocal reductions (Rosencranz, 1986).

Under such circumstances, it may be in the interests of wealthier countries to underwrite at least part of the cost that economically disadvantaged countries would incur in making investments that would ameliorate conflicts over the use of international resource domains. The recently instituted practice of swapping debt for environmental commitments is an example of such a practice. A more basic and less direct strategy would attempt to improve the general economic condition of poorer countries, for example by reducing trade barriers to enhance their trade opportunities.

5.2 Access to technologies

Less developed countries have been sensitive to situations in which more advanced countries possess technologies that give them significant advantages in exploiting international resource domains. They maintain that these domains are the 'common heritage of mankind', and thus belong to the entire community of states, regardless of their level of technological development. This type of issue has been raised in regard to mining of the deep seabed and the launching of satellites into outer space.

States with technological means of exploiting these domains advocate policies that would impose few if any constraints on their operations, but they have recognized the need for international regulations to prevent interference from other users. However, in attempting to negotiate such rules, they have repeatedly encountered a large, unified bloc of Third World countries, caucusing as the Group of 77.

In return for recognizing and legitimizing the uses of the developed countries, the Group of 77 have made a variety of requests: technological assistance or transfers at affordable prices that would enable them to exploit the commons; participation in joint projects with the advanced countries; future access guaranteed by a priori allocations; or a share in the proceeds that the advanced countries glean from the resource domain.

5.3 Vulnerability to collateral damage

Agreement on international policies is sometimes more difficult because of disparities in vulnerability to collateral damage. For example, states that are upwind in an airshed generally 'export' more air pollutants than they 'import'. Thus, they accrue fewer gains from international regulations relative to the costs they incur than do their downwind neighbors who are more heavily victimized by emissions from other states. Likewise, coastal states with off-shore fishing operations have a much greater interest in preventing overharvesting of nearby fisheries than do states which send out distant-water fleets that can be readily moved to other regions.

An incongruence of interests rooted in relative collateral damage is difficult to resolve unless there are other issues, such as international trade or military security, on which the roles are reversed and the perpetrator of the collateral damage is dependent on the cooperation of the victim. Lacking reciprocal vulnerability, the victim state can only hope that those causing the collateral damage will recognize the obligations implied by principles of international custom such as state responsibility and good neighborliness.

5.4 Historical uses of the resource domain

Inequalities in the previous use of an international resource domain complicate the task of agreeing upon new limitations. Established heavy users may be willing to accept a specified percentage reduction, but historically light users, especially less developed countries, may contend that it is only fair that they be free to reap the benefits from an intensified use of the domain.

The problem is illustrated by China's refusal to agree to reductions in production of CFCs mandated by the Montreal protocol on preserving the ozone layer, even with its provision of a ten-year grace period for less developed countries. In an effort to make refrigerators more widely available, Chinese production of CFCs has been growing at approximately 20% annually during the 1980s and a tenfold increase was projected by the year 2000. Even then, however, Chinese production per capita would be only one-fifth of the level of the United States if it were to achieve the 50% reduction by 1998 mandated in the Montreal agreement ('Chinese to increase CFC production', 1989, p. 21). China and other less developed countries have indicated repeatedly that they will agree to CFC reductions only if the developed countries assist them in adopting environmentally harmless substitutes (Tyson, 1989, pp. 1–2).

5.5 Previous national restraints

Percentage reductions in the use of resource domains are regarded as being unfair to countries that have already reduced their impact on a unilateral basis. Those who took the lead in acting responsibly argue that they should be given credit for what they have already accomplished. Otherwise they would shoulder a heavier burden than the 'free riders', who can satisfy international standards on percentage reductions by taking a relatively inexpensive first step to reduce usage.

The United States opposed the 1988 ECE protocol limiting emissions of nitrogen oxides, arguing that it should be given credit for reductions over the past 10 years achieved by requiring catalytic converters on automobiles. Had this argument been accepted, the United States would have been allowed a 10–20% increase while other parties to the protocol would be required to freeze their emissions at 1987 levels by 1995 (Ågren, 1988, pp. 1–2). Ironically, the United States continues to be the world's leading per capita emitter of nitrogen oxide pollutants, in part because of policies such as relatively low gasoline taxes and a massive program of highway constructions, which have encouraged a much heavier reliance on motorized vehicles for transportation. Thus, achieving regulations that are perceived to be equitable by all major users of international commons will continue to test the skills of negotiators and the willingness of governments to negotiate.

5.6 Previous exclusive claims

Conflicts are more difficult to resolve when some users claim exclusive rights to parts of an international resource domain. Such claims were made to develop oil fields in the Gulf of Mexico in 1946, followed by unilateral declarations of expanded territorial waters and fishery zones as far out as 200 miles by many states. Several states have long-standing, and in some cases overlapping, claims to pie-shaped segments of Antarctica. A group of equatorial states issued the Bogota Declaration in 1976, which proclaimed exclusive rights to the sections of the geostationary orbital arc lying above their countries. Few other countries have supported them in this claim and there is little the Bogota group can do to deny access to the orbit by other states.

Past experience suggests how difficult it is to persuade countries to relinquish such claims, although they may be willing to make some compromises with the international community. The provision for EEZs in the new ocean law legitimizes most of the unilateral claims of coastal states, but does not confer all prerogatives associated with territorial waters. Claims to Antarctica were held in abeyance in the Antarctic Treaty of 1959, but increasing interest in the mineral wealth of the continent may make it necessary for the treaty states to attempt again to resolve this difficult issue.

6. Conclusions

This chapter highlights some of the types of conflict that arise from incompatible uses of international and global commons, which are likely to become more intense with growing pressures worldwide to increase use of these resource domains. It also calls attention to several alternative strategies that could be adopted by the international community to address these conflicts, while pointing out that the task of reaching agreement to implement any one of them raises additional conflicts of interest that must first be resolved.

The prospects of managing these conflicts would be very bleak were it not for several developments that have been changing the character of world politics. The first is a noticeable lessening of the Cold War tensions between East and West and a more general, worldwide tendency to turn away from the counterproductive behaviors associated with power politics. Second, there are promising signs of a broad-based willingness to enhance the role of the United Nations as an institutional mechanism for addressing global problems. Third, the severity of environmental problems, especially those pertaining to preservation of the atmosphere, and the need to develop international public policies to address them, is now recognized by major national leaders from both the political right and left.

Environmental problems, including those that arise from the use of international commons, pose a special challenge to peace researchers. Scientific knowledge of the consequences of human activities for the natural environment has been mushrooming, but effective international action to ameliorate or adapt to these changes entails devising strategies for resolving international conflicts that threaten to thwart efforts to bring about constructive change.

Note

1. A resource domain is an area or a region, defined broadly, that encompasses something that is of use to human actors and over which some form of jurisdiction can potentially be exercised. For example, the pasture in Hardin's analogy is a resource domain which contains grass which is useful for grazing cattle. Similarly, the seabed is a resource domain on which are located nodules which are resources. The atmosphere is a domain which serves as a sink for pollutants. Outer space is a resource domain in that it encompasses useful locations for positioning communication satellites.

References

Ågren, C., 1988. 'The NOx debacle', *Acid News*, no. 2.

'Chinese to increase CFC production', 1989. *Environment*, vol. 31, no. 2.

Hardin, G., 1988. 'The tragedy of the commons', *Science*, vol. 162, no. 3859.

Oakerson, R., 1986. 'A model for the analysis of common property problems', in National Research Council (ed.), *Proceedings of the National Conference on Common Property Resource Management*. Academic Press: Washington DC.

Rosencranz, A., 1986. 'The acid rain controversy in Europe and North America: a political analysis', *Ambio*, vol. 15, no. 1.

Tyson, J.L., 1989. 'Why China says ozone must take back seat in drive to prosperity', *Christian Science Monitor*, 23 March.

Wijkman, P.M., 1982. 'Managing the global commons', *International Organization*, vol. 36, no. 3.

4 The Control of Atmospheric Pollution: Is There an East–West Conflict?

Tapani Vaahtoranta

1. Introduction

Is it worthwhile looking for conflicts of interest when the common environment of mankind has to be protected? In fact, we are often told that environmental cooperation should be easier than cooperation on many other international issues. For example, from the perspective of functionalists, environmental problems 'should offer a new basis for human cooperation and a new unifying principle, creating the possibility of a global morality and a new planetary politics' (Knelman, 1972–3, p. 35). David Mitrany himself believed that functionalism could be used as a method to solve international environmental problems. There seem to be two reasons for this optimism. Environmental protection appears to be a relatively non-political issue area, while competition and conflict prevail in other spheres. It may also seem feasible to separate environmental affairs from political and other interstate conflicts.

This view is not entirely wrong. Important agreements to reduce international atmospheric pollution have been signed, even though, since the early 1970s, grave concern has characterized not only forecasts regarding the man–nature relationship but also the political capacity of mankind to curb environmental degradation.

However, international environmental protection is not purely technical problem-solving. As in other issue areas, conflicts of interest among states characterize environmental diplomacy. These conflicts can have two sources. The external source involves issues other than environmental protection, for example, 'high' politics among states. The characteristics of environmental issues are the internal source of conflict.

The purpose of this chapter is to elaborate upon the potential external and internal causes of an East–West conflict as far as the control of atmospheric pollution is concerned. An external cause of the conflict, the Cold War, is first discussed. Three potential internal causes of the conflict are then outlined: differences in ecological vulnerability, in the level of technological progress and in the nature of political systems. In conclusion, changes to the path of conflict among the industrialized states are described.

2. The Cold War as a cause of the conflict

Despite optimistic expectations, the separation of environmental cooperation from political conflict is not always possible. Conflicts related to the Cold War, in particular, have often hindered international environmental protection.

For example, in the 1970s, the German question made international, regional and bilateral environmental protection difficult. Owing to the controversy over the status of the GDR, the Soviet Union and the Eastern European countries, with the exception of Romania, stayed away from the UN Conference on the Human Environment in 1972, giving, it is true, assurances that they were not opposed to environmental protection as such. Regional cooperation for the protection of the Baltic is another example. The states bordering on the Baltic were able to sign the agreements of the 1970s on the protection of the living resources and the marine environment of that sea only after the FRG and other states recognized the GDR in 1973 (Rytövuori, 1980, p. 85). Finally, the establishment of a Federal Environment Office in West Berlin in the 1970s interrupted efforts by the German states to control the bilateral pollution of the rivers running between them (Füllenbach, 1981, p. 144). The border dispute between the German states is another political obstacle which in the 1980s prevented them from reaching an agreement on purifying the River Elbe.

In like manner, the USA and the Soviet Union concluded the agreement on Cooperation in Environmental Protection in 1972 during the height of the *détente* period. In 1976 they were working together on 39 different environmental projects. When tension began to rise by the end of the decade, environmental cooperation also suffered. Only after the great powers were again ready for better political relations, more active environmental cooperation became possible. The summit meeting in Geneva in 1985 led to the signing of a new bilateral agreement on environmental cooperation between them (Ziegler, 1987, pp. 136–7). According to a US official, 'now [1985] that we seem to be returning toward a détente attitude between the two governments, we are free to move forward on the environment' (Shabecoff, 1985).

Since 1985 environmental cooperation between the United States and the Soviet Union has been improved, together with the strengthening of political ties. The leaders of both countries issued a joint statement during the June 1990 presidential summit, in which they expressed 'serious concern about the health of the global environment and their commitment to expand US-Soviet cooperation in the field of environmental protection and global change' (International Environment Reporter, 1990, p. 246).

The Cold War as an obstacle to effective East–West environmental cooperaiton seems now to be disappearing. The *détente* of the 1970s was not sustainable, but there may be structural changes taking place in the international system, as well as changes in Soviet and American perceptions of each other, that could strengthen the present *détente* (see Williams, 1989). The fragmentation of power among states is moving the international system from bipolarity to multipolarity, at least as far as economic resources are concerned. As a result, the structural pressure to great-power rivalry may be weakened. In a world where there are other threats to national well-being, the great powers may be less preoccupied by each other. In other words, the changing distribution of power and influence is mitigating the security dilemma between the USA and the Soviet Union. Besides, the influence of ideology on both Soviet and US foreign policies may be declining. If *glasnost* and *perestroika* continue, the American image of the Soviet Union as an 'evil empire' bent on global domination could change, and with it the American perception of threat.

It is, of course, possible that certain events could derail *détente* and precipitate a return to the Cold War. One such obstacle is the turmoil in Eastern Europe. The failure of *perestroika* in the Soviet Union could have fatal consequences for the *rapprochement*. The German question is also important to the relationship between the great powers. Nevertheless, it seems that the gradual erosion of bipolarity offers new opportunities for the Soviet Union and the USA to move to a more cooperative approach. It thus seems unlikely that the US–Soviet rivalry would become a major obstacle to East–West cooperation on protecting the environment.

In contrast, the conflicts of interest related to environmental issues themselves are more apt to create East–West controversies over environmental protection.

3. Environmental issues as a cause of the conflict

It is sometimes expected that environmental degradation might lead to a situation where states would regard it as constituting a 'common danger' to the viability of the earth (see, e.g. Caldwell, 1972, p. 5). In fact, it is suggested that a new holistic view of environmental problems is already emerging, one that is causing governments to be concerned about the welfare of the world as a whole. In other words, *realpolitik* is being replaced by 'ecopolitics', which means that ethical considerations are being injected into new international politics and that they could become more significant determinants of international behavior (Pirages, 1978, p. 1).

Though this view is an exaggeration, it is true that the growing severity of international atmospheric pollution is a process change (Nye, 1988, pp. 249–50) which is making the world more interdependent. Ecological interdependence is of political significance in that being affected by outside forces restricts the autonomy of the state.

In principle, a state can seek to protect its environment unilaterally or together with other states. In most cases, however, no state can prevent pollutants from moving into its territory. In most cases, however it is either impossible or very costly to prevent adverse consequences of international pollution. Interdependence is thus making the unilateral approach outdated. It is increasingly difficult for an individual state to protect its environment by unilateral action in a world of ecological and economic interdependence. A state's own reductions, even though achieved at great expense, can correct only part of the problem if others do not introduce corresponding regulations. As a result, international atmospheric pollution stimulates a strong 'demand' for international cooperation among states (Keohane, 1982).

The need for environmental cooperation does not necessarily mean that effective cooperation is possible. The sources of difficulty in environmental cooperation are twofold. First, although mankind faces common environmental problems, the international system lacks a central authority which could articulate the common interest and act upon it. The interests that shape collective measures in the face of common problems are national rather than international or global. Second, international environmental protection is not purely technical problem-solving; conflicting interests are typical of it. Because states are different and not equally affected by environmental degradation, they perceive different needs for environmental protection. In short, environmental cooperation is not so harmonious as is sometimes assumed.

Three factors, in particular, shape the attitudes of a state in the control of international pollution: its vulnerability to pollution, its ability to reduce emissions, and the characteristics of its domestic political system. Ecological vulnerability is important. For some time it has been apparent that national interest could be harnessed to the cause of environmental protection if environmental problems became sufficiently exacerbated. The more serious problems become, the more they would threaten the core of national interest, national security. To reduce environmental damage, states would have to make adaptive changes in their foreign policies (Shields and Ott, 1974, pp. 642–7). The problem from the perspective of cooperation is that states are not equally affected by pollution. Thus it is in the interest of a victim state, which is ecologically vulnerable, to try to strengthen its position by reducing pollution. It is apt to be a 'pusher' in environmental diplomacy. But why should less vulnerable states be eager to promote strict controls on international pollution? They are more apt to be 'draggers'.

Economic and technological capabilities also affect state behavior in the matter of environmental protection. The more emission reduction would cost a state, the more reluctant it is to support international regulations. If environmental protection is cheap, it is easier to be a pusher state and strive for emission controls.

The environmental foreign policy of a state also depends on its political system. Generally speaking, each society has been led by a 'pro-growth' complex, which is biased toward economic growth at the expense of adverse side-effects such as environmental degradation. As it has not yet been in the self-interest of pro-growth élites to invest in environmental protection, they must be induced into doing it. For this purpose, political mobilization of the citizenry and the responsive decision-making system is important. Since citizens are likely to suffer from environmental degradation before élites do, those systems that allow citizens to influence policies have the advantage. In other words, the democratic states that allow citizen groups to raise the question of environmental quality and build an effective organization to press for pollution control are more apt to implement effective environmental policies than states with a more authoritarian government (Kelley et al., 1976, pp. 286–91; Gottweis, 1988).

4. The line of conflict in the 1980s

The main line of conflict in the negotiations that led to the signing of the Helsinki Protocol, which obliges states to reduce sulfur emissions by 30%, and the Montreal Protocol, which obliges states to reduce the production and consumption of chlorofluorocarbons (CFCs) by 50% in two stages, was between the Western states. Both the pushers and the draggers were capitalist states of the West.

As to sulfur emissions, 10 states—Austria, Canada, Denmark, the Federal Republic of Germany, Finland, France, the Netherlands,

Norway, Sweden and Switzerland—promised at a conference in Ottawa in 1984 to reduce emissions by 30% by 1993. This 'Ottawa Club' was soon joined by Belgium, Liechtenstein, and Luxembourg, while Italy, the UK and the USA, in particular, expressed the views of the draggers (Lang, 1986, p. 269; Prittwitz, 1986, pp. 68–9; Wetstone and Rosencranz, 1984, pp. 88, 148). The Helsinki Protocol was signed in 1985. Three major sulfur emitters—the USA, the UK and Poland—have not yet signed it.

During the negotiations on the protection of the ozone layer, Austria, Canada, Denmark, Finland, Norway, Sweden, Switzerland and the USA met in Toronto in 1984 to push a control protocol on the production and consumption of ozone-depleting CFCs. In addition to this 'Toronto group', the Netherlands was ready in 1984 to accept a protocol that would significantly reduce the use of CFCs in aerosols. France, Italy, Japan and the UK were the most conspicuous dragger states at that time. All major producers of harmful substances signed the Montreal Protocol in 1987.

In the case of negotiations on both sulfur emissions and the production and consumption of CFCs, the socialist states were 'bystanders'. They did not ally with either the pushers or the draggers. When the agreements were ready for signing, the socialist states usually went along with them.

Since the signing of the protocols the line of conflict has been changing. The Western states have become increasingly eager for more effective regulations, while it has been more difficult for the Soviet Union and former socialist states to accept the tightening of restrictions on harmful production and emissions.

The change is most evident in the negotiations on the protection of the ozone layer. It is noteworthy that the European Community agreed in March 1989 to call for a complete ban on ozone-depleting production in a conference which was arranged by the British government in London. The Soviet delegates opposed new regulations. In the Helsinki Declaration, issued in May 1989, the representatives of 81 countries and the European Community agreed to a total phase-out of CFCs by the year 2000 and to a phase-out of other ozone-depleting substances as soon as possible. Even though the Soviet Union joined the Declaration, it considered the total phase-out difficult.

Many Western states are also reducing their sulfur emissions more than the Helsinki Protocol obliges them to. The states that formed the Ottawa Club to press for the international 30% reduction agreement, and Luxembourg, have unilaterally reduced or are planning to reduce sulfur emissions more than the Helsinki Protocol requires. The policy of the USA may also be changing. President George Bush issued a clean air bill in 1989, according to which sulfur dioxide emissions would be halved by the end of the century.

The former socialist states find it more difficult to cut sulfur emissions. The Nordic states have explored the possibility of signing a new multilateral agreement that would oblige states to reduce emissions by 50%, but the Soviet Union and the Eastern Eurpean states have been reluctant to go along with such an agreement.

5. The different German states

The recent enthusiasm of the FRG for a reduction in atmospheric pollution is a good example of the 'greening' of the West. Earlier, the FRG resisted international efforts to control acid rain and preserve the ozone layer, but has recently actively promoted effective international regulations. It is noteworthy that unlike other states that push for such rules, notably Canada, the Netherlands and the Nordic states, the FRG is one of the world's greatest emitters of air pollutants. All three factors—vulnerability to atmospheric pollution, economic wealth and the availability of new technologies, and public pressure—seem to have contributed to the FRG's change of policy on environmental protection.

First, with regard to acid rain, the area of central Europe comprising Germany, Belgium, the Netherlands, Poland and Czechoslovakia has the highest acidity precipitation in Europe. In the mid 1980s half of West German forests were seriously affected by acid rain, more than is reported in any other European country (Kauppi et al., 1987, p. 28). Only in the Netherlands is severe forest damage more widespread than in the FRG ('ECE . . .', 1987).

Though the damage to the West German forests dates back to the 1960s, *Waldsterben* (forest death) did not cause public alarm until the beginning of the 1980s, when the phenomenon spread dramatically. This awareness coincides with the change in the FRG's policy toward new international targets for sulfur dioxide emission reductions. The sudden about-face of the FRG was first evident at a conference in Stockholm in 1982, when it abandoned the drag state camp and declared its support for the establishment of an international program for controlling sulfur dioxide throughout Europe.

Second, the ability to produce new compounds for CFCs seems to explain the change in West German policy on ozone depletion. The FRG first opposed proposals offered by the Nordic countries, the Netherlands and Canada of large reductions in CFC production. In 1987, however, West German officials issued a statement that the FRG would aim at a near-total elimination of CFC production and emissions by the year 2000. The government would begin the reduction by concentrating on the aerosol industry. The aerosol industry was willing to abide by the plan, having already gone a long way toward the elimination of all but essential aerosol uses of CFCs, with further reductions in sight (Dickman, 1987).

Similarly, the USA continued to oppose international regulations on other than aerosol uses of CFCs, until in 1986–7 it began a drive to end all uses. At about the same time, the first reports appeared in the press on the development of new substitutes for CFCs. In 1988, Dupont, a US-based company which is the largest producer of CFCs, announced that it would be able to produce a substitute for CFCs in a few years and accordingly supported 'an orderly transition to a total phaseout' of the most harmful CFCs ('Ozone . . .', 1988).

Third, public pressure on policy-making seems to explain why increasing vulnerability and technological advances affected West German environmental foreign policy so quickly. Through its open political system citizens have been able to make environmental protection a salient political issue and ultimately to influence the decision-making process.

The greening of West German environmental foreign policy becomes even more evident when it is compared with the attitude of the GDR to acid rain. The GDR signed the Helsinki Protocol in 1985. It did not, however, ratify the Protocol since, according to an East German official, it did not intend to reduce its sulfur emissions by 30% by 1993 (Michélsen, 1989a), to say nothing of deeper cuts.

Invulnerability to acid precipitation cannot be the reason for the GDR's policy on sulfur emissions. Although it is difficult to find data on the sulfur deposition in the former GDR, the country is unquestionably located in that area where acidity precipitation is the highest in Europe.

Why did vulnerability affect the attitude of the FRG to acid rain but not that of the GDR? Two factors seem to explain this difference between the German states. First, the level of technological progress was lower in the GDR than in the FRG. In plain terms, the GDR wasted energy and in doing so produced a great quantity of harmful discharges. The FRG used energy almost three times more efficiently than the GDR. This fact, together with the dependence on brown coal and an almost complete lack of emission control, explain why East Germany emitted 35 kilograms of sulfur per 1,000 dollars of GNP, while the FRG emitted only 5 kilograms (Chandler, 1987, pp. 182, 187).

Second, the political systems in the German states were different.

While the Greens may have had more political influence in West Germany than in any other country, it was much more difficult for the citizenry of the GDR to affect environmental policies. Public pressure for more effective environmental protection has been suppressed in at least two ways in East Germany. It was difficult even to obtain information about the state of the environment since the matter was kept secret. Besides, it was illegal to found environmental groups (Michélsen, 1989b).

6. Current political changes in the socialist states

The environmental policies of the FRG and the GDR may not have been representative of all the Western and Eastern industrialized states. Nevertheless, they point to general differences between these countries in the willingness and the ability to reduce atmospheric pollution. These differences might, in the near future, have led to East–West controversies over environmental protection if important changes had not taken place in the socialist states.

In the Soviet Union, these changes result from the current reform policy, *perestroika* and *glasnost*, which aims at increasing the efficiency of the Soviet economy. It is important from the point of view of environmental protection that more room for citizen initiatives and public participation is required for the economic reform to succeed. In fact, the political mobilization of citizens has already affected Soviet domestic environmental policy: polluting factories have been shut down and plans involving adverse ecological effects abandoned. Clearly, the Soviet Union has become more willing to acknowledge that serious environmental problems exist in its territory, and to manage them.

The reform policy seems also to be affecting the environmental foreign policies. In October 1989, the Soviet Union signed an agreement with Finland on controlling bilateral transboundary air pollution. According to the agreement, sulfur emissions will be reduced by 50% by 1995 in Finland and the Murmansk area, Karelia, the Leningrad area and Estonia. Further reductions in sulfur and nitrogen emissions should be agreed upon in 1993. Hungary is another example. The Hungarian Parliament decided in October 1989 to abandon the Nagymaros–Gabcikovo hydroelectric project as a result of greatly increased domestic opposition to it. Poland, too, seems to be increasingly willing to reduce its emissions of pollutants, which cause transboundary acid rain and degrade the Baltic Sea, but cannot afford to invest in environmental protection.

The political reform in the Soviet Union and in the former socialist states of Eastern Europe is crucial to their willingness to protect the environment and to clear obstacles to cooperation in Europe. Willingness alone is not, however, sufficient. States must also be able to reduce emissions. Therefore, the success of the economic reform in the Soviet Union and the countries of Eastern Central Europe is crucial. Also, there is a need to establish financial and other mechanisms to enable these states to meet the requirements of European environmental protection.

References

Caldwell, Lynton K., 1972. *In Defense of the Earth: International Protection of the Biospere*. Indiana University Press: Bloomington.

Chandler, William U., 1987. 'Designing sustainable economies', in Linda Starke (ed.), *State of the World 1987: A Worldwatch Institute Report on Progress Toward a Sustainable Society*. W.W. Norton: New York.

Dickman, Steven, 1987. 'West Germany strides towards CFC elimination by 2000', *Nature*, vol. 327, 14 May.

'ECE Report: European forest damage', 1987. *Acid News*, no. 3, October.

'Emissions: Europe: yesterday, tomorrow', 1987. *Acid News*, no. 3, October.

Füllenbach, Josef, 1981. *European Environmental Policy: East and West*. Butterworth: London.

Gottweis, Herbert, 1988. 'Politik in der Risikogesellschaft', *Österreichische Zeitschrift für Politikwissenschaft*, vol. 17, no. 1.

Kauppi, Pekka, Kaarle Kenttämies, Seppo Oikarinen and Raisa Valli, 1987. *Happamoituminen Suomessa: Maa ja metsätalousministeriön Happamoitunisprojektin yleiskatsaus*, Sarja A, no. 57. Ympäristöministeriö, Ympäristö- ja luonnonsuojeluosasto. Helsinki printing: Helsinki.

Kelley, Donald R., Kenneth R. Stunkel and Richard R. Wescott, 1976. *The Economic Superpowers and the Environment: The United States, the Soviet Union and Japan*. W.H. Freeman: San Francisco.

Keohane, Robert O., 1982. 'The demand for international regimes', *International Organization*, vol. 36, no. 2.

Knelman, F.H., 1972–3. 'What happened at Stockholm?'. *International Journal*, vol. 28, no. 1.

Lang, Winfried, 1986. 'Luft und Ozon—Schutzobjekte des Völkerrechts', *Zeitschrifte für Ausländisches Öffentliches Recht und Völkerrecht*, vol. 46, no. 2.

Michélsen, Thomas, 1989a. 'DDR största svavelspridaren i Sverige om tre år: Brunkolet gigantiskt hot mot miljön', *Dagens Nyheter*, 6 August.

Michélsen, Thomas, 1989b. 'Fakta om miljö hemlighetstämplas', *Dagens Nyheter*, 12 August.

Nye, Joseph S., Jr, 1988. 'Neorealism and neoliberalism', *World Politics*, vol. 15, no. 2.

'Ozone: a close call', 1988. *International Herald Tribune*, 29 March.

Pirages, Dennis, 1978. *The New Context for International Relations: Global Ecopolitics.* Duxbury Press: North Scituate.

Prittwitz, Volker, 1986. 'Die Luft hat keine Grenzen: Das Problem der weiträumige Luftverschmutzung', in Peter Cornelius Mayer-Tasch (ed.), *Die Luft hat keine Grenzen: Internationale Umweltpolitik, Fakten und Trends.* Fischer Taschenbuch: Frankfurt am Main.

Rytövuori, Helena, 1980. 'Structures of détente and ecological interdependence: cooperation in the Baltic Sea area for the protection of the marine environment and living resources', *Cooperation and Conflict*, vol. 15, no. 2.

Shields, Linda P. and Marvin C. Ott, 1974. 'The environmental crisis: internationalf and supranational approaches', *International Relations*, vol. 4, November.

Wetstone, Gregory S. and Armin Rosencranz, 1984. *Acid Rain in Europe and North America: National Responses to an International Problem.* 3rd pr. The Environmental Law Institute: Washington DC.

Williams, Phil, 1989. 'US–Soviet relations: beyond the Cold War?', *International Affairs*, vol. 65, Spring.

Ziegler, Charles E., 1987. *Environmental Policy in the USSR.* Frances Pinter: London.

5 The Conflict of Interests Between the Environment and Military Strategy in Northern Waters and the Arctic

Lassi Heininen

The relationship between the devastation of the environment and military strategy is present in military action. This is especially apparent in major naval accidents, as can be seen, for example, in the sinking of the Soviet Mike class nuclear-powered attack submarine (SSN) in April 1989; the submarine sank to an approximate depth of 1,800 metres in the Norwegian Sea 180 kilometres from Bear Island— probably carrying nuclear depth charges, anti-submarine warfare missiles, nuclear tipped torpedoes as well as some sea-launched cruise missiles and two liquid-metal cooled nuclear reactors (*The Sinking of the Soviet Mike Class Nuclear Powered Submarine*, 1989). The risk of devastation to the environment would possibly cause a conflict of interests between nations and states, even between allies. In Northern waters and in the Arctic such cases are acute.

1. Expanding the term 'traditional security'

Accidents similar to the one mentioned above are, in themselves, a good reason to expand the terms 'traditional security' and 'national security' by adding the dimension of environmental security and environmental protection. The hypothesis presented here is that military strategy, especially military presence and any action, will have an environmental effect, causing threats and risks[1] to the land and sea areas of the Arctic even in peacetime, as has happened already.

This is not to say, however, that acute pollution and other potential environmental risks and problems in the Arctic should be underestimated: obviously an oil spill in the Arctic seas constitutes a total and acute catastrophe for marine flora and fauna.

What have been seen as threats to traditional security are also changing, or may have already changed, from the global threat of nuclear destruction to the fear of potential global environmental catastrophes—although the study of a possible nuclear winter has also previously been included. The term 'security' is no longer solely the straightforward, traditional, national dimension of security, envisaging mainly military threats—today we hear terms such as 'interdependence', 'common security', 'sustainable development' and 'environmental security'. These are all global and go far beyond limited national thinking. An important factor to understand in this debate is that nuclear arms pose a growing risk, and that this risk is far out of proportion to the amount of security which they may provide for mankind ('The relationship between disarmament and development', 1982, pp. 15, 20, 157).

Actual and potential effects and risks of military strategy to nature and to the whole environment have not always been seen as a problem. Military presence and action—especially nuclear weapons, nuclear tests and nuclear-powered ships and submarines—already constitute a great risk to nature and to people in certain regions, especially in the Pacific, but in the Arctic as well. I therefore speak of a relationship between 'benefits and costs'; the 'benefits' of armaments and armies to the security of people and their lives, compared to the 'costs' of wasting natural resources and human knowledge, and the environmental effects of the arms race.

We can also study the question of security by looking at conflicts and contrasts in the Arctic. Military strategy is in contrast with nature and the human environment and with everyday life, especially where the ways of indigenous peoples are concerned. It also runs counter to the reasonable and sustainable utilization of natural resources, e.g. oil and gas drilling in the Barents Sea. This is especially true of areas where the utilization of natural resources requires the most sophisticated environment-sparing technology.

2. Military strategy in Northern waters

Since the beginning of the 1980s both the Soviet Union and the United States have developed increasingly sophisticated naval and air weapons and arms systems, especially nuclear arms, and placed them in Northern waters. According to Greenpeace data there are, in the seas surrounding Northern Europe, more than 5,700 nuclear warheads on 494 warships,[2] which are using 62 naval bases, docks, nuclear stores, airfields and command, control, communication and intelligence (C^3I) centres (Greenpeace, 1988, pp. 20–1, 40–5).

The Arctic and Northern waters are strategically important areas. Geographically they form a vast region, the military use of which has been made possible by modern arms technology, almost completely, not only under the surface but also under the ice. The nuclear powers are extending their military potential to the Arctic Ocean by strategic submarines (SSBNs), and nuclear-powered attack submarines (SSNs), the latter to search for the SSBNs. The US maritime strategy of keeping a forward-based presence of its navy has, together with the modernization of the Soviet navy and the Soviet naval bases on the Kola Peninsula, played a part in enhancing the strategic role of Northern waters. Thus the nuclear question of Northern Europe has changed during the past few years: the presence and transit of nuclear-powered and nuclear-armed warships have become an important challenge to security and to security policy, and in this way to the environmental protection of the countries of Northern Europe and of the Arctic as well (Heininen, 1988, pp. 57–64).

3. Forms of military existence in the Arctic

This chapter does not deal with the environmental effects of modern warfare or the influences of environmental warfare on fauna, flora and the human environment, but only with the effects of routine military existence during peacetime. By military existence I mean, primarily, military presence and activities, that is, daily routine, and also, more generally, the whole arms race process. In the context of my subject, the Arctic, there are only limited land areas and broader water areas where military presence and activity are felt. Recently, the Arctic, and Northern waters as well, have become a military area for both conventional and nuclear arms.

Environmental effects in the Arctic and in Northern waters are caused by military presence, or deployment itself, and military activities or action (excluding warfare)—routine military activities during peacetime. Johan Galtung uses the concept of 'military preparation' similarly, separating it from 'military action', by which he means warfare and its influences (Galtung, 1982, pp. 26–30). Environmental effects can be either potential, mainly nuclear risks, or actual, such as pollution, which is taking place constantly.

3.1 Military presence

Military presence and preparation in peacetime is in itself a threat to fragile Arctic nature and the human environment and thus to the region's everyday life. The use of land areas for bases and garrisons and other military purposes is a present threat which brings pollution by oil, gasolines, chemicals and other toxic substances.

Examples of military presence and deployment in the Arctic are:

(i)   Areas used for military facilities such as bases and garrisons.
(ii) Radar bases on the fjelds and islands, cables on the sea bottom and on land, i.e. the whole command, control, communications and intelligence (C^3I) system.
(iii) Ports in coastal areas.
(iv) Airports on the slopes of fjelds and in the valleys.
(v)   Large areas of wilderness, fjelds and sea for military maneuvers, e.g. in the North Calotte, the Kola Peninsula and Northern Canada.
(vi) Facilities and weapons for testing nuclear arms and cruise missiles and for low-level flights.

3.2 Military action

Military action (excluding warfare) in the form of 'necessary' training during peacetime occupies large land and sea areas and produces environmental pollution. Military action occurs in many forms, for example:

(i)   Maneuvers in land and sea areas, including naval accidents and incidents.
(ii) Nuclear and missile tests, e.g. anti-submarine warfare (ASW) tests in Nanoose Bay.
(iii) Low-level flights in the wilderness, above seas and also near towns and villages, e.g. in Nitassinan Goose Bay in Canada there are today 7,000 low-level flights per year by NATO jets,[3] and a projected 20,000 in the near future (Bellefeur, 1989; *The Canadian Peace Report*, Spring 1989, pp. 4–5).
(iv) Constant patrolling at sea, in the air and on land areas, involving nuclear warheads and reactors on ships and in submarines.
(v)   Visits of warships to ports and aircraft to airports.
(vi) The dumping of old munitions into the sea or in or on the ground.

The relevant point is that military strategy has an acute effect in the Arctic and Northern waters all the time. Military presence and action are also a risk or threat to the everyday life of indigenous peoples and other northern inhabitants; it influences way of life, state of mind and livelihood. Most northern indigenous peoples have been suffering from the military use of northern regions; military maneuvers disturb fishing and reindeer herding, noise disturbs people and animals, and the creation of national borders, e.g. in the North Calotte, separate families.

4. Nuclear accidents

Nuclear accidents involving nuclear-powered and armed vessels are the most dangerous category of military accidents. They represent great potential environmental risks in that their effects can be totally disastrous, long-lasting and far-reaching. The risk of naval disasters is universal and a cause of concern in all oceans, so I will survey this problem generally and then concentrate specifically on Northern waters.

According to data on naval accidents, between 1945 and 1988, the major navies have had a total of 1,276 accidents.[4] Among them are 212 documented accidents involving nuclear-powered ships and submarines (between 1954 and 1988) (Arkin and Handler, 1989a). Currently, there are 552 nuclear reactors on warships, most of them in submarines, and 23 others on icebreakers and 1 on a research ship—in comparison with approximately 430 commercial nuclear reactors ('Nuclear Notebook . . .').[5]

Due to these accidents there are at least 50 nuclear warheads and 11 nuclear reactors in 3 US and 4 Soviet nuclear-powered submarines in the oceans today (including the reactors of the Mike-class submarine) (Arkin and Handler, 1989b, p. 22).

Almost half of the accidents have happened in the Atlantic Ocean and over 300 in the Pacific. The Arctic seas, including the Arctic Ocean and the seas surrounding the Antarctic, have been the scene of only 2% of the total number of accidents (excluding accidents in 1989).[6]

The majority of naval accidents in Northern waters have been fires and groundings, but 2 nuclear submarines have also sunk and other accidents have involved 16 nuclear-powered submarines and 6 diesel-powered submarines. There have also been collisions between warships and between warships and fishing vessels, as well as at least 2 nuclear reactor disasters aboard Soviet nuclear-powered icebreakers: a reactor meltdown on a Lenin icebreaker in the late 1960s and almost another on a Rossia icebreaker in Murmansk harbor (Arkin and Handler, 1989a, pp. 33, 72).

Other types of military accident have also taken place in the Arctic: in January 1968 the crash of a B-52 bomber carrying four 1.1-megaton hydrogen bombs polluted large land, snow and ice areas near Thule in Greenland with the deadly plutonium of ignited radioactive fuel. The Danes and Inuits cleaned up the pollution area and 1.5 million tons of land, snow, ice and water were removed, but according to rumours, 12 of the 16 kilograms of plutonium contained in the 4 bombs were not recovered. Now, 20 years after the accident, many members of the rescue team have cancer, have died of cancer, or suffer from sterility and chronic fatigue (Heininen, 1988, pp. 115–16; *Time*, 8 February 1988, p. 15).

Most naval accidents have been caused by technical problems or a human factor. In many cases there is a human error behind a technical problem. There are also other reasons such as sabotage or arson, use of drugs (e.g. in US nuclear submarines), suicides, lack of skill (e.g. in Soviet nuclear submarines). Modern technology has not been able to stop or even decrease the number of naval accidents and there are, and will be, other naval accidents and risks of increasingly dangerous nuclear disasters (Arkin and Handler, 1989b, p. 20).[7]

It is thus clear that accidents in navies are not rare. Arkin and Handler's figures are probably not complete, since such facts are military secrets. Generally there is no public information on naval nuclear forces available from any of the five nuclear-weapon powers apart from the USA. Certain naval activities, especially those concerning submarines and nuclear weapons, are among the most secret military activities (Fieldhouse and Taoka, 1989, pp. 9–10). The whole idea behind the SSBNs and SSNs remains secret, the result being 'out of sight, out of mind' for most people. Secrecy and the problem of verification are the greatest obstacles to naval arms control. The navies of the nuclear powers have attempted, with success, to conceal naval accidents. During recent years, however, researchers and the public have become concerned and interested in the risks such accidents involve.

An important point is that accidents have happened in routine naval operations during peacetime, not just during crises or wartime, and that nuclear weapons are routinely carried on all US and Soviet aircraft carriers, logistics-support ships, submarines and most surface warships that have the capacity to carry them (Fieldhouse and Taoka, 1989, pp. 137–40).

Naval nuclear accidents and incidents may also be the beginning of larger incidents: conflicts, crises, escalation and even accidental nuclear war between the nuclear powers, although there are agreements to prevent this. The oceans are the only area where the nuclear weapons of the Soviet Union, the USA and the other nuclear powers can come into concrete contact and thus into conflict with each other. About 23 accidents have been documented between vessels of the USA or Britain and the Soviet Union (Arkin and Handler, 1989b, pp. 23–4). These accidents have happened, and other similar naval accidents could happen, because of the monitoring of vessels at sea or during routine operations off the coasts of other countries or in the 'game of chicken', which has, above all, military purposes (for more details, see Ball, 1988, pp. 306–7).

With regard to naval accidents there is also an element of misuse in the 'neither confirm nor deny' policy of the major nuclear navies, especially in the maritime strategy of the USA. The accident at Thule and that at Ticonderoga near Okinawa in the Pacific in December 1965 provide strong evidence for the violation of the nuclear–weapon–free policy of both Denmark and Japan (White, 1989, pp. 33–5).

5. Effects on marine nature

Nature in the Arctic—both flora and fauna—is extremely fragile; the same holds true for the marine environment in that region. Despite this, the influences of military presence and action are not known or have not been studied enough, although debate on the environmental effects of nuclear accidents has started. There exist some documented scientific data concerning the environmental changes and contamination caused by nuclear waste and nuclear tests, but more and longer range follow-ups are clearly called for.

There are also other kinds of radioactive contamination of the seas such as the dumping of low- and medium-active nuclear wastes, accidents during the sea transportation of nuclear wastes and routine fuel release and accidents at nuclear power plants. Radioactive isotopes and contamination are, however, only a part of the main sources of pollution in the seas together with oil, poisons (such as DDT, PCB) and heavy metals (Sanger, 1986, pp. 100–3); there is evidence that radioactive fallout is affecting the Arctic. In the mid-1960s there was a peak in the radioactive contamination of lichen, reindeer meat and the Sa'mi herders in the Lapplands of Fennoscandia as well as of the water of the Baltic Sea by Caesium-137. This increase was due to nuclear weapon tests in the atmosphere, in Novaja Zemlja.[8]

Caesium-137 and Strontium-90 are effectively absorbed in the ground and in lichen from the air, snow and rainwater. In many places lichen forms 30–60% of the winter diet of the reindeer and in this way certain wild beasts, Sa'mi herders and other men who eat reindeer meat are affected. The situation was the same in Alaska between 1962 and 1970; in this case with caribou meat and lichen (for more details see Nieminen, 1987; Mackay, 1987). The 77 nuclear weapon explosions in Novaja Zemlja are part of the effects which have caused illness to Chukchi in the Chukchi Peninsula; indigenous Chukchi eat large amounts of reindeer meat and absorb a hundred times as much Caesium-137 as people who do not eat this meat (radioactive radiation has been twice the normal amount during the last 25 years) (*The Los Angeles Times*, 11 August 1989).

6. Potential conflicts of interests

A general conflict of interests, in addition to the tension and juxta-position of the Soviet Union and the USA (and NATO) and their military policies and navies,[9] is already present in the Arctic: a conflict of interests between military strategy and civil activities, e.g. the utilization of natural resources, environmental protection, multi-lateral cooperation and the way of life of indigenous northern peoples.

The relationship between armed conflict and the environment can appear in three different forms:

(i) Environmental destruction as a consequence of armed conflict.
(ii) Environmental degradation as the cause of military conflict (e.g. global climatic changes).
(iii) Environmental changes as a contribution to armed struggle, adding new dimensions to existing conflicts (Holst, 1987, p. 9).

In addition, there are four political conflicts of interests also with NATO and inside the Soviet Union—some potential, and sometimes obvious—over the potential environmental risks of military accidents and the pollution caused by military presence and activities.

6.1 Iceland

Situated in the middle of the GIUK gap, Iceland is strategically important to NATO, but during crises and wartime it is one of the main naval battle areas. Fish is the most important renewable re-source and source of livelihood for Iceland and also the most important export as far as the economy of Iceland is concerned. Since 'the Icelandic people—an island nation—make their living to a great ex-tent on the living resources of the sea' (Statement by His Excellency Mr Thorsteinn Pallsson, 1988, p. 6), they are always ready to defend the marine resources of the nearby seas. This is enough to create a conflict between the maritime strategy of the USA and the national interests of Iceland.[10]

The US navy is present in the Norwegian Sea at all times with nuclear-powered and armed submarines and ships,[11] which need service in ports near the Norwegian Sea. The USA and Iceland have the Defense Agreement of 1951 and America has the air force base of Keflavik in Iceland, with American aircraft, soldiers and radar. However, there have been no visits of US warships to the ports of Iceland since the year 1985—none of the aircraft carriers or nuclear submarines of the US navy, or other nuclear state's navy, has visited an Icelandic port—although one reason for this could be their poor port facilities.

There have been frequent security policy debates in the Icelandic Parliament since World War II and citizens have been concerned over NATO membership, the US air base in Keflavik and, generally, about nuclear weapons. In 1964 the Icelandic foreign minister made a statement prohibiting the stationing of nuclear weapons on Icelandic soil; this was later confirmed. After the debate of 1985 concerning the stationing of nuclear weapons and port visits, the then foreign minister stated that the policy of a nuclear weapon-free Iceland included warships, and thus 'warships carrying nuclear weapons have no authority to enter Icelandic waters nor put into Icelandic ports' (White, 1988, p. 21).

The Icelandic government and Icelanders are primarily worried over the naval activities of the Soviet Union in nearby seas. In Iceland there has been suspicion that the Nordic nuclear weapon-free zone will not be sufficient for the security of the country. For this reason the Icelandic Parliament passed a resolution on disarmament including plans for a comprehensive zone in Northern Europe to cover the sea areas (Jónsson, 1989, p. 19). Iceland has often emphasized the need for a larger nuclear weapon-free zone than that proposed by other Nordic countries.

One of the main concerns of Icelanders is the potential risk to the marine ecosystem and thus to the livelihood of Iceland (Pallsson, 1988, pp. 6–7; 'A report to the Althing by Steingrimur Hermannsson', 1988, p. 10; Gunnarsson Arni, 1990, pp. 8–10) which is caused by accidents in submarines or on surface warships carrying nuclear weapons and reactors. This concern emerged during the 1980s.[12] There is a conflict of interests between the policy of Iceland and the maritime strategy of both the Soviet Union and the USA, because Iceland does not want nuclear-powered and armed warships in its ports or in the surrounding waters. However, the USA has unofficially adapted itself to this policy.[13]

Today, probably mainly due to the two accidents to Soviet submarines in Northern waters, Iceland is ready to stop the arms race at sea, to place limits on the transit of nuclear-powered and armed vessels, and generally interested in naval arms control (Pallsson, 1988, p. 7; Jónsson, 1989, p. 20; Grimsson, 1989). One conclusion to be drawn is that environmental threats and risks, at least in the nearby seas, can be a motivation for arms control.

6.2 The Northwest Passage

There has been a conflict of interest between Canada and the USA concerning the freedom of the high seas, which is manifested in the dispute over the status of the Northwest Passage, which runs through the Canadian Arctic archipelago. An American oil tanker, the *Manhattan*, in 1969, and a US Coastguard icebreaker, the *Polar Sea*, in 1985, traveled through the Northwest Passage. After the voyage of the *Manhattan*, Canada proclaimed the Arctic Waters Pollution Prevention Act (1970), which was the first such act for the environmental protection of sea areas (*Maclean's*, 19 August 1985, pp. 16–19; 'The North and Canada's international relations', 1988, p. 40). The purpose of the Act was to control the movement of such foreign vessels as formed a risk of disaster to the ecosystem of these fragile Arctic waters (Degenhardt, 1985, pp. 219–20; Hakapää 1988, pp. 29, 46).

In a debate after the transit of the *Polar Sea*, the main point of concern in Canada was the sovereignty of the country over its Arctic archipelago and waters; but there was also concern for the fragile environment of the Arctic.[14] Canada established straight baselines in 1985 and this strengthened its legal status concerning these waters ('The North and Canada's international relations', 1988, pp. 42–3; Pharand, 1988).

It is not only the surface ships of the USA and other countries[15] which are causing concern in Canada by transiting via Canadian internal Arctic waters, but also nuclear-powered and armed submarines in general, the naval strategies and operations of the Soviet Union, and of the USA as well (see, e.g. McGee 1988, p. 90). The common opinion regarding the competition of the superpowers is that, in a crisis, Canadian Arctic waters would become a field of operations for Soviet SSNs, maybe SSBNs and at least long-range sea-launched cruise-missiles (SLCMs). There is, however, no relevant reason or evidence that Soviet SSBNs, or even the Soviet SSNs, have used, or are using, these waters (Miller, 1989, pp. 10–11; Cox, 1988, pp. 22–4; 'The North and Canada's international relations', 1988, p. 7; Factsheet 7, 1989; Harbron, 1988a, p. 97). On the other hand, there is evidence that US nuclear-powered and armed submarines have used Canadian

Arctic waters, transiting via Canadian internal Arctic waters, on their way to the North Pole. For example, nuclear-powered Sturgeon class SSNs have completed more than 30 secret 30–50-day missions in the Arctic Ocean. This was, ironically enough, one reason for the decision of the government of Canada to acquire 10 or 12 nuclear-powered submarines of its own in order to patrol the Canadian Arctic waters (Harbron, 1988a, pp. 97–8; Harbron, 1988b; Factsheet 7, 1989)—a plan which has, however, been shelved (*Helsingin Sanomat*, 28 April 1989).

In 1988 the governments of Canada and the USA signed an agreement on Arctic cooperation; this includes a pledge by the USA 'that all navigation by US icebreakers within waters claimed by Canada to be internal will be undertaken with the consent of the Government of Canada' and a principle of protection and research cooperation on the marine environment in the Arctic (Agreement between the Government of Canada and . . ., 1989). Whether this is the end of the dispute is not yet certain, because the USA has not recognized Canadian sovereignty over the Canadian Arctic archipelago and waters ('The North and Canada's international relations', 1988, p. 42).

6.3 The Murmansk district

There is a new, and not yet manifest, potential conflict of interests within the Soviet navy in the Murmansk district.

On the Kola Peninsula and especially in the Murmansk district, there are many large naval bases and airfields with a large number of nuclear-powered and armed warships and nuclear-armed airplanes (Ries and Skorve, 1986; Purver, 1988, pp. 2–11), but there are also important, populated towns, e.g. the town of Murmansk and large industrial centers.

Due to the intensive use of the rich natural resources of the Kola Peninsula by old-fashioned technology during the last 50 years there are today enormous environmental problems and pollution. If future plans for industry, for example the mining of minerals and drilling of oil and gas in the ocean shelf, are to be completed, the Soviet Union will need high technology and the cooperation of other countries. Thus it is easy to understand that the inhabitants of the Murmansk district are worried about the present, enormous environmental problems on the Kola Peninsula, and also about the potential threats brought by the greater utilization of natural resources and enlarged industrial areas. Many people, especially environmentalist and peace groups, but also Nenets people, are also concerned about the environmental risks inherent in all military equipment, especially underground nuclear tests in Novaja Zemlja, and nuclear weapons and reactors in submarines and surface ships, but also reactors in nuclear-powered icebreakers, in the naval bases and ports near the town of Murmansk.[16]

6.4 Military versus civilian interests

For several years there has been a conflict of interests, constantly increasing, between the military strategy (including naval presence, transit and activities) of the Soviet Union and the USA and civil activities, mainly oil and gas drilling and transportation in the Barents Sea. Nuclear disasters such as the accident to the Mike-class submarine would be fatal to the whole marine ecosystem of the Barents Sea due to the cold and icy waters and the shallowness of the sea. The influences of major nuclear accidents would damage large seafishery areas, and also affect oil and gas drilling.

This conflict of interests is already visible between the naval strategy of the Soviet Union and petroleum strategy—the planned production of offshore oil and gas by Norway and the Soviet Union as well as some multilateral joint ventures in the near future.[17] Thus not only natural conditions such as the cold, the ice and the shallowness of the sea, but also civilian economic activities, especially those of multilateral cooperation, will, or at least should, affect military strategy by decreasing military presence and operations in the Barents Sea (Bergesen et al., 1987, pp. 57–8 and 83–4).

However, the idea of military strategy and naval doctrine contains one main problem: the secrecy of the arms race, the armies and other military elements including naval and other military accidents and the influence of these accidents. This, in itself, is in conflict with the need for openness or *glasnost* in modern society and in productive cooperation, e.g. in environmental protection between nations, and one natural forum for it would be the international process on environmental protection in the Arctic. Although in civilian sea transportation, there is much precise, at least theoretical, advice concerning safety, nuclear-powered and armed submarines travel in many dangerous waters and in bad conditions, due to the need for secrecy.

It is interesting that foreseeable and potential conflicts or contrasts between the environment and military strategies in the Arctic are not derived solely from the East–West confrontation and competition between the Soviet Union and the USA, but also from national interests such as sovereignty and national livelihood as well as the use of natural resources and cooperation. It is obvious that military strategies, assuming that military presence and activities will increase or remain at an intensive level, are in conflict with nature and the environment and will be in conflict with present, and possibly broader future multilateral cooperation in the Arctic.

Notes

1. There are two concepts used here: that of threat and that of risk. Maybe the concept of risk is better than that of threat, which is a more psychological term.
2. The total number of nuclear vessels today is estimated at 747 (two years ago the figure was 941 vessels and 15,600 warheads) ('Nuclear notebook . . .', 1988); this consists of submarines and other warships, which have about 14,600 nuclear warheads and 552 nuclear-powered reactors ('Nuclear notebook', 1990). According to two evaluations, the high seas are constantly patrolled by 30–4 strategic submarines with 3,100–4,000 nuclear warheads. They are arranged at periods of 70 days; part of the time in transit and part on station. At all times there are some submarines in transit, some on station and the rest in training or on sea trials (UN Study on the Naval Arms Race, 1985, p. 71; Fieldhouse and Taoka, 1989, pp. 93–4).
3. Low-level flights create noise, sonic booms, aircraft emissions and microwaves and in this way concern for environmental and public health. There are also other difficulties such as the risk of crashes and other accidents to people, especially to children (noise has been found to cause behavioral disturbances such as insomnia and nightmares). In this case the people concerned are mostly Innues living on their own lands (Wadden, 1988, pp. 4–5).
4. The distribution of this figure is: 406 accidents on surface ships, 359 in submarines, 228 on aircraft carriers, 182 on logistic support ships, 75 on amphibious warships and the remainder on other warships.

   The twelve major categories of naval accidents are: collisions (456 documented cases), fires (267), groundings (130), explosions (114), equipment failures (98), sinkings (75 including 27 submarines), weather conditions (65), propulsion accidents (59), ordnance accidents (non-explosive) (54), aircraft crashes on ships (34), flooding (27), and miscellaneous (80). See Arkin and Handler, 1989a.
5. Naval nuclear reactors are divided in the following way: 167 in SSBNs, 78 in SSGNs, 265 in SSNs and the rest in surface ships ('Nuclear notebook . . .', 1990).
6. The sites of 170 accidents, most of them English warships, are unknown; however, most have taken place in the Atlantic Ocean.
7. An example of high-tech risks are the 6 recent accidents with the US Navy's combat aircraft proving rather well how vulnerable modern jets

are. These 6 accidents were only part of the 12 major naval accidents in the US Navy within 3 weeks in October–November 1989 (*Newsweek*, 27 November 1989, pp. 31–2).

 8. There were 417 nuclear weapon tests in the atmosphere between 16 July 1945 and 5 August 1963 (the total of nuclear explosions is 547) and 180 of these 417 tests were carried out by the Soviet Union, 77 of them in Novaja Zemlja between the years 1957 and 1962 (*SIPRI Yearbook 1987*, table 2A.2., p. 54; Westing, 1980, pp. 121 and 142, table 6.3).

 9. The Soviet Union and the USA are superpowers which have a powerful naval presence especially in Northern seas. However their navies are asymmetrical in character and reflect different geopolitical and economic backgrounds. This is one reason for the lack of naval arms control and disarmament (Fieldhouse and Taoka, 1989, pp. 6–7, 29).

10. See the 'cod wars' in the mid-1970s between Iceland and Britain and the proclamation of Iceland as an exclusive economic zone of 200 nautical miles in 1975 (Armstrong, Rogers and Rowley, 1978, p. 228).

11. The USA has 25 SSBNs at sea every day, the Soviet Union 15 SSBNs and the other nuclear-weapon states 7, i.e. there are 47 SSBNs with more than 5,100 warheads ready, of which 30–4 SSBNs with about 4,000 warheads are on patrol and ready to fire (Fieldhouse and Taoka, 1989, pp. 93–4; UN Study on the Naval Arms Race, 1985, p. 71).

12. For example Prime Minister Hallgrimsson did not mention the dimension of the risk of disaster in his speech in the UN General Assembly in 1978 (see Hallgrimsson, 1978).

13. For more details see: Heininen, 1988, pp. 77–8; Pallsson, 1988, p. 5; Gunnarsson Gunnar, 1989.

It is interesting to note that this conflict of interests between Iceland and the USA is not so sharp and tense as the similar conflict between New Zealand and the USA, though the reason is the same: the prohibition of port visits of nuclear-powered and armed warships because of the environment. There are some differences between the case of Iceland and that of New Zealand: Northern seas are strategically more important for the USA than the seas around New Zealand and New Zealand's nuclear-free legislation prohibits visits of all kinds of nuclear weapons and nuclear materials to its ports (Heininen, 1988, pp. 42–3).

14. Some headlines from Canadian newspapers and magazines: 'Testing the Northwest Passage. The U.S. icebreaker *Polar Sea* challenges Canada's Arctic sovereignty' (*Alberta Report*, 12 August 1985, p. 26); 'U.S. offers Canada pollution' (*The Gazette*, Montreal, Wednesday, 31 July 1985); 'Who rules the Arctic?' (*Edmonton Journal*, 15 February 1987).

It is interesting that in 1987 58% of those who answered the questions of the Canadian poll thought that the USA was threatening Canada's legal right to the Arctic and only 37% thought that the Soviet Union was the threat (*The Globe and Mail*, Saturday, 15 August 1987).

15. The total number of full transits of the Northwest Passage between the years 1903 and 1987 is 45: 29 by Canada, 11 by the USA and 5 by vessels of

other countries ('The North and Canada's international relations', 1988, pp. 12–13).

16. Discussions at the seminars of the Festival for Peace and Environment in Murmansk 26–8 July 1989 and the comments of the peace activists of the Murmansk district in the seminar with Nordic peace groups in Murmansk 26 January 1991. See also the interview of Aleksander Vyutjéjskij, who is the representative of the Nenets people in the Soviet parliament (Nordisk Kontalket, 1990, pp. 29–31).

17. For example the Barents Sea gas project, which is exploring the production of gas in the Shtockmanovskoye gas-field on the shelf of the Barents Sea; and in which American, Finnish and Norwegian partners are cooperating with the Soviet Ministry of Oil and Gas Industry (Jumppanen, 1990).

References

'Agreement between the Government of Canada and the Government of the United States of America on Arctic cooperation', 1989. Canada, Treaty Series 1988, no. 29. Ottawa.

Alberta Report, 1985. 12 August.

Arkin, William M. and Handler, Joshua, 1989a. 'Naval accidents 1945–1988', *Neptune Papers*, no. 3, June.

Arkin, William M. and Handler, Joshua, 1989b. 'Nuclear disasters at sea, then and now', *The Bulletin of Atomic Scientist*. July/August.

Armstrong, Terence, Rogers, George and Rowley, Graham, 1978. *The Circumpolar North*. Cambridge: Methuen & Co.

Ball, Desmond, 1988. 'Nuclear war at sea', in Steven E. Miller and Stephen Van Evera (eds), *Naval Strategy and National Security*. Princeton: Princeton University Press.

Bellefeur, Guy (the chief of Innues in Labrador), 1989. A Speech to the Nordic Peace Conference in Montreal 15–17 September.

Bergesen, Helge Ole, Moe, Arild and Östreng, Willy, 1987. *Soviet Oil and Security Interests in the Barents Sea*. London: Frances Pinter.

The Canadian Peace Report, 1989. Spring.

Cox, David, 1988. 'Canada's changing defence priorities: comparing notes with the Nordic states', in Kari Möttölä (ed.), *The Arctic Challenge. Nordic and Canadian Approaches to Security and Cooperation in an Emerging International Region*. London: Westview Press.

Degenhardt, Henry, W., 1985. *Maritime Affairs—A World Handbook. A Reference Guide to Maritime Organizations, Conventions and Disputes and to the International Politics of the Sea*. A Keesing's Reference Publication. London: Longman.

Edmonton Journal, 1987. 15 February.

Factsheet 7, 1989. Security: Canada and the Arctic'. March. Canadian Institute for International Peace and Security.

Fieldhouse, Richard and Taoka, Shunji, 1989. *Superpowers at Sea. An Assessment of the Naval Arms Race*. SIPRI, Strategic Issue Papers. Oxford: Oxford University Press.

Galtung, Johan, 1982. *Environment, Development and Military Activity. Towards Alternative Security Doctrines.* Stavanger: Universitetsforlaget.

The Gazette, 1985. Montreal, 31 July.

The Globe and Mail, 1987. 15 August.

Greenpeace, 1988. *Atomfrit Hav.* April.

Grimsson, Olavur Ragnar, 1989. Hur kan Island stäka den gemensamma säkerheten? *Gemensam säkerhet i Norden. Hot och svar.* Oslo: Nordiskt forum för säkerhetspolitik.

Gunnarsson, Arni, 1990. Det islandske folks utkomme i fare. *Nordisk Kontakt* 5/90, pp. 8–10.

Gunnarsson, Gunnar, 1989. '"Neither confirm nor deny": the case of Iceland'. 6 December (mimeo).

Hakapää, Kari, 1988. *Uusi kansainvälinen merioikeus.* Helsinki: Lakimiesliiton Kustannus.

Hallgrimsson, Geir, Prime Minister of Iceland, 1978. To the 10th Special Session of the General Assembly Devoted to Disarmament, Monday, 29 May. Permanent Mission of Iceland to the United Nations.

Harbron, John D., 1988a. 'Canada's independence at sea'. *Proceedings*, vol. 114/3/1021.

Harbron, John D., 1988b. 'Yankee sub, go home!'. *Proceedings*, vol. 114/8/1026.

Heininen, Lassi, 1988. *Pinnan alla kytee. Pohjois-Euroopan ydinaseongelman merelliset ympäristöuhat.* Rauhantutkimus tänään, no. X. Tampere: Suomen Rauhantutkimusyhdistys.

Helsingin Sanomat, 28 April 1989.

Holst, Johan Jörgen, 1987. 'Security and the environment: a preliminary exploration. Security and the environment exploring some key issues of our times'. In Report on a workshop organized by the Royal Norwegian Ministry of Defence in support of the World Commission on Environment and Development, 27–9 October 1986, Oslo.

Jónsson, Albert, 1989. *Iceland, NATO and the Keflavik Base.* Öryggisma'lanefnd. Reykjavik: Icelandic Commission on Security and International Affairs.

Jumppanen, Pauli, 1990. Discussion in Helsinki, 2 January.

The Los Angeles Times, 11 August 1989.

Mackay, Louis, 1987. 'Chernobyl's fallout on the reindeer people', *END Journal*, no. 28/29.

Maclean's, 19 August 1985.

McGee, John E., 1988. 'Call to Action in the Arctic'. *Proceedings*, vol. 114/3/1021.

Miller, Steven, E., 1989. 'The Arctic as a maritime theater' (mimeo).

Newsweek, 27 November 1989.

Nieminen, Mauri, 1987. 'Porot ja säteily'. The Research Society of Lapland, *Yearbook XXVIII*, Rovaniemi.

Nordisk Kontakt, 1990. Norden bes om stötte for prövestans på Novaja Semja. Samtale med nenetsenes representant i det överste sovjet. *Nordisk Kontakt*, 12/90, pp. 29–31.

'The North and Canada's international relations', 1988. The Report of a Working Group of the National Capital Branch of the Canadian Institute of International Affairs. March. Ottawa.

'Nuclear notebook: nuclear weapons at sea', 1988. *Bulletin of Atomic Scientists*, vol. 44, no. 7.

'Nuclear notebook: nuclear weapons at sea', 1990. *Bulletin of Atomic Scientists*, vol. 46, no. 7.

Pallsson, Thorsteinn, 1988. 'Islannin ulko- ja turvallisuuspolitiikka. Esitelmä Paasikivi-seurassa 9.6.1988', *Paasikivi-seuran monistesarja*, no. 77, Helsinki.

Pharand, Donat, 1988. 'Canada's sovereignty in the Arctic'. *'The North and Canada's international relations.* Appendix A.' Ottawa: Canadian Arctic Resources Committee.

Purver, Ronald, 1988. 'The militarization of the Arctic'. A paper given to TAPRI Workshop on Alternative Security and Development in the Arctic Regions, Ivalo, Finland, 14–16 November (mimeo).

'The relationship between disarmament and development', 1982. United Nations, *Study Series 5*. New York.

'A report to the Althing by Steingrimur Hermannsson, Minister for Foreign Affairs of Iceland', 1988. *Foreign Affairs*, February.

Ries, Tomas and Skorve, Johnny, 1986. *Investigating Kola. A Study of Military Bases Using Satellite Photography.* London: Brassey's Defence Publishers.

Sangèr, Clyde, 1986. *Ordering the Oceans. The Making of the Law of the Sea.* London: Zed Books.

The Sinking of the Soviet Mike-class Nuclear-powered Submarine, 1989. A preliminary technical assessment of the potential radioactive inventory release into the marine environment associated with the Soviet Mike-class nuclear-powered attack submarine accident, Norwegian Sea, 7 April. Large and Associates: London. (Report Ref. LA RL 1866. 12 April 1989. Commissioned by Greenpeace International.)

SIPRI, 1987. *Yearbook 1987: World Armaments and Disarmament.* Oxford: Oxford University Press.

Statement by His Excellency Mr Thorsteinn Palsson, Prime Minister of Iceland, 1988. In the General Debate of the Third Special Session of the General Assembly of the United Nations Devoted to Disarmament, 2 June.

Time, 8 February 1988.

UN Study on the Naval Arms Race, 1985. *Report of the Secretary-General.* General Assembly, A/40/535, 17 September.

Wadden, Marie, 1988. 'His Labrador business'. *Peace & Security*, Autumn.

Westing, Arthur H., 1980. Warfare in a Fragile World. Military Impact on the Human Environment. Arthur H. Westing, SIPRI, London: Taylor & Francis.

White, Robert, E., 1988. 'Nuclear ship visit policies and ship visit data for 55 countries: a brief analysis'. *Scientists Against Nuclear Arms.* Auckland (mimeo).

White, R.E., 1989. 'The neither confirm nor deny policy: oppressive, obstructive, and obsolete'. December. Draft (mimeo).

6 Political Aspects of an Environmental Conflict: The Case of the Gabcikovo–Nagymaros Dam System

Judit Galambos

1. Introduction

This chapter is a case study on the political dimension of an environmental conflict arising over the construction of the Gabcikovo–Nagymaros dam system on the Danube by Czechoslovakia and Hungary (see Figure 6.1). From a political point of view this is a very interesting and complex case: it has caused both domestic and international conflicts. The course of these conflicts was strongly influenced by the political democratization process: the controversy gradually focused on the very nature of the political system in Hungary.

The case also provides a unique opportunity to compare decision-making in different political regimes and during different historical periods, since it has a long history, in which three neighboring countries—Czechoslovakia, Hungary and Austria—have played the central roles. Furthermore, through the course of events the clashes of national, political, ecological, economic, and bureaucratic interests can be studied.

2. Description of the project

The Gabcikovo–Nagymaros Barrage System (hereafter called GNBS) under construction between river kms 1696 and 1862 on the Danube consists of three dams and two hydroelectric power plants. The Danube was to be dammed at Hrusov/Dunakiliti to flood an area of 60 square kilometers, ending in Bratislava. (From Dunakiliti down to the mouth of the Ipoly the Danube forms the common border between Hungary and Czechoslovakia.) The water level of the reservoir would then rise

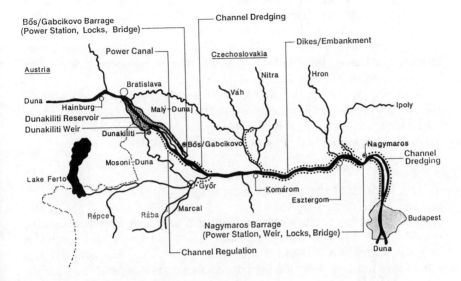

Figure 6.1   Plan of the Gabcikovo–Nagymaros dam system (GNBS)

6.5 m above the ground at Dunakiliti. The water was to be routed downstream from the dam to a hydroelectric plant, the second dam and lock at Gabcikovo via a 17 km-long canal running parallel to the Danube 5 km within the borders of Slovakia. The walls of the 300–650 m wide canal were to be built to a height of 9–18 m above the surrounding gravel and sandy terrain and the canal was to be lined with asphalt and special plastic to prevent seepage. The Gabcikovo plant was planned to have 8 turbines and a capacity of 720 megawatts. From the Gabcikovo plant, the water course was to be routed back in an 8 km-long canal to join its old bed at Palcikovo/Szap. The whole canal was to be on Slovakian territory and international water traffic was planned to be diverted to the canal from the 31 km-long section of the 'old' river-bed, where only 50–200 cubic meters per second would flow instead of the present 2,000 average.

From the mouth of the canal 100 km downstream, the Danube bends southward, entering a steeper valley by Nagymaros in Hungary. This was planned to be the site for another hydroelectric plant, the third dam, with the capacity of 158 megawatts. The Nagymaros plant was planned to work continuously, but producing only two-seventh of the total energy produced by the whole system. The Gabcikovo plant was intended to work only in peak hours: during the rest of the day most of the water of the river would be retained in the reservoir at Dunakiliti. In peak consumption hours this water would be allowed to surge through the turbines at Gabcikovo. This would in turn create great changes in the water level—5 m under the plant—which would be compensated by the Nagymaros dam.

According to the Czechoslovakian–Hungarian bilateral agreement, the two countries would equally share the construction work and costs, and, after completion, also the electricity produced (3,775 million kilowatt-hours per year) (Fisher, 1989; Kien, 1984).

3. The history of the project

In the nineteenth century certain leading Czech nationalists sought to create a united Czech-Slovakian state, whose borders would reach the Danube, which would connect their country with the sea and with the other Slav nations. For this purpose the new state was to incorporate large ethnic Hungarian territories around the river. The possibility of realizing this plan arose at the Paris Peace Conference, at the end of World War I, where it was settled that the southern border of the new state—created from Bohemia and Slovakia, which had earlier belonged to the Austro-Hungarian Monarchy—would extend to the Danube, and thereby incorporate ethnic Hungarian territories into Czechoslovakia, even though the Czechs and Slovaks had originally wanted to get large Hungarian territories also on the other side of the Danube.

In the political situation that prevailed during the inter-war period Czechoslovakian politicians were afraid that they would not be able to keep the ethnic Hungarian territories and the Danube. Therefore the country's authorities did their utmost to mix the Hungarian population along the Danube with Slovaks. They did not give up their policy after World War II: Hungary was pressed by the victorious Great Powers to come to an agreement with Czechoslovakia on a 'mutual exchange of population', and this in turn meant that Prague was allowed to expel as many Hungarians from Slovakia to match the number of Slovaks moving from Hungary to Czechoslovakia. However, the 'exchange of population' failed to effect the de-Magyarization of the riverside to the extent planned, since the number of Hungarians was much greater in Slovakia than the number of Slovaks in Hungary. The disruption of this ethnic bloc will certainly be more effectively completed by the construction of the diversion canal of the GNBS by the year 2000.

Czechoslovakia also tried at the Paris Peace Conference of 1946 to acquire possession of a territory *vis-à-vis* Bratislava, on the Hungarian side of the Danube. Had Czechoslovakia succeeded, this would have made a unilateral diversion of the Danube by the Slovaks possible. However, neither state was given such a right at the peace conference and Slovakia got only half of the territory it had claimed (Kien, 1984).

This historical background helps us to understand why the Hungarians have had less enthusiasm for the joint project than the Czechs and Slovaks. Soviet pressure and communist ideology, however, facilitated the realization of the Czechoslovakian aspirations after 1948.

From 1948 the Soviet Union played a dominant role in the Danube Committee, which had long urged the construction of a barrage system on the joint Czechoslovakian–Hungarian section of the Danube, in order to eliminate its shallows. The improvement of navigability has mainly been a Soviet interest, since Soviet ships have transported the greatest amount of goods in this section of the Danube. But this alone would not have made the construction of a by-pass canal necessary: this has been exclusively a Slovakian interest, because in this way Czechoslovakia could completely obtain a 31 km section of the Danube; the canal would contribute to the disruption of the ethnic Hungarian bloc on the Slovakian side of the Danube and Bratislava would become a big international port (Kien, 1984).

Joint planning commenced in the early 1950s. After the so-called planning committees of the two countries had approved the plans of the dam system, the appropriate standing committee of COMECON also approved them in 1961. They were signed on governmental level by the two countries concerned in 1963 (Kien, 1984).

The communist ideology and the communist economic system were decisive factors in dragging the Hungarians into the joint project. In the years after the war even leading water management specialists emphasized the serious technical, economic and ecological limitations to utilizing water power in Hungary. But in the early 1950s, the gigantic projects of the Soviet Union, such as the hydroelectric plants at Stalingrad and Khuibishev on the river Volga, set the examples to be followed (Vargha, 1981).

'Transformation of nature' was an important element of communist —Stalinist—ideology, according to which mankind was able 'to conquer nature' with the help of central planning. Since the 'capitalist' categories of profitability and economic efficiency were disregarded, even these limitations concerning 'transforming nature' ceased to exist during the Stalinist regime. That is why, in the 1950s, Hungary built up a huge steel industry without the necessary raw materials, produced cotton in spite of unfavorable natural conditions for cotton-growing, and started to build hydroelectric plants on the rivers flowing through its plains. Soviet 'experts' and their Hungarian students provided the decision-makers with the necessary 'scientific' proofs and data for these decisions.

During the debates conducted in the 1950s on dams and hydroelectric plants, the water management bureaucracy had gradually to change its standpoint. If it had continuously emphasized the obstacles to such plans, it would never have gained the support and money of the energy sector which, for the same expenditure, could have built a thermal plant power station with a capacity twice as great as that of the hydroelectric plant (Vargha, 1981).

In the communist economy, the various ministries and state-owned companies competed with each other for the limited resources available from the state budget. According to communist ideology bankruptcy in a planned economy is impossible: this can only happen under the 'chaotic' conditions of capitalism. Moreover, bankruptcy of a state-owned company would mean that the management, the controlling bureaucracies or the planners had made serious mistakes. This, however, is something that nobody wants to admit and therefore the company is granted extra resources from the state to ensure its survival. Economic considerations play no role whatsoever in the redistribution mechanism. On the contrary, the firm which shows the worst financial balance will be rewarded.

This is also true for large investments: once construction has been started, it is easy to get more and more resources to complete the project. Therefore it is better to underestimate considerably the costs and difficulties at the outset, in order to influence decision-makers in favor of the project. If new difficulties should arise in the course of realization, there would be no cause for concern: the same bureaucracy would remove them in order to ensure employment for a growing number of people—especially bureaucrats—for a long time (Borson, 1989).

This is how the Hungarian water management bureaucracy conducted itself. In order to obtain the necessary support and resources, planners and the water management establishment started to emphasize the energy production side of the project. Since energy production from the planned hydroelectric plants simply could not be competitive because of the unfavorable natural conditions, the costs of the investment had to be curbed through manipulation: for example, the investment costs were reduced by the amount of money provided by the energy sector; other sectors were charged with the expense of the necessary additional investments (e.g. sewage treatment), etc. (Vargha, 1981).

In the 1960s professional disputes about the ecological and economic problems continued among specialists, but even most of those with reservations concerning the concrete plans wanted to participate in some kind of construction of a hydroelectric plant, and therefore had to be satisfied with the version enjoying the most political support.

After 1968 preparations for the realization of the project were speeded up: in Czechoslovakia the conservative wing of the party hierarchy re-centralized its power after the Soviet invasion. The new First Party Secretary, Gustav Husak—being a Slovak—favored specifically Slovak schemes such as the GNBS. In the early 1970s, the two sides worked out a joint plan of investment and a draft contract. The oil crisis of 1973 raised questions concerning energy supply in both countries, thus giving further impetus to the realization of the plans.

While the peace treaties after the two wars had determined the middle line of the navigational route on a certain section of the Danube as the state borders between Czechoslovakia and Hungary, the by-pass canal would divert this route, thus changing the conditions under which the borders had been set. It had to be decided whether the border should be moved to the middle line of the new navigational route i.e. the by-pass canal. According to the joint investment plan of 1973, the question of borders was to be settled in a separate treaty. However, in 1973 the Czechoslovakian side proposed 'the re-examination of the necessity and expedience of the proposed modification of the border'. After 3–4 years of high-level negotiations, the Hungarian party leadership withdrew its demand for the modification of the border and approved the 31 km-diversion of the Danube's water into Slovakia and the construction of the dam system. In 1977 the two governments signed a bilateral agreement on the construction of the GNBS (Kien, 1984).

4. The controversial features of the project

Before going any further in this account of how the conflict evolved both within and between the participating countries, attention should be given to the alleged benefits and drawbacks of the project, since they became objects of vehement dispute.

The planners and the supporters of the project sought to justify its construction employing the following arguments:

(i)   The GNBS would produce electricity at peak consumption times, replacing the air-polluting brown coal operated power stations in Slovakia.

(ii)   The presumed energy needs of the Hungarian economy could not be met without the energy produced by the hydroelectric stations of the GNBS.

(iii) The dam would protect the Danube lowlands from floods.

(iv)   The project would result in improved navigability, connecting the two countries with the Danube-Rhine-Main Canal.

(v)   The project would promote the irrigation of agricultural lands above the dams.

(vi)   In the latter phase of construction it was often argued that abandonment of the project was impossible because the money already invested would be lost—this is still the main argument in Slovakia, which has almost completed construction at Gabcikovo —and further high costs would be caused by restoration and the payment of compensation to Austria and Czechoslovakia, not to mention the political and economic harm caused to Hungary by not fulfilling its international legal obligations.

But as was seen in the previous section, there were also hidden benefits as follows:

• the satisfaction of Slovak national aspirations;
• the satisfaction of Soviet navigational interests;
• the provision of the water management experts and bureaucracies with employment, power, financial resources and professional careers;
• the demonstration of the power of the regime, in the same way as pyramids, cathedrals, triumphal arches and skyscrapers symbolize power.

In the 1950s and 1960s dams and hydroelectric plants were regarded as reasonable solutions for energy production and for irrigation. Their harmful environmental and social consequences became known and public only later (see Hildyard and Goldsmith, 1984), but even today hundreds are being built all over the world. Apart from the detrimental effects mentioned in Hildyard's book, others will also be caused by the GNBS because it is being built on a plain and because this section of the Danube constitutes an especially beautiful natural and historical landscape. The main counter-arguments against the GNBS have been summed up in the following:

(i)   The GNBS will jeopardize the freshwater supplies of millions of people. The possibility for water production through bank-filtration—the cheapest way of gaining drinking water—will be completely lost in the area. The GNBS also threatens contamination of the area's subterranean water reserves, the largest in Europe.

(ii) The GNBS will destroy valuable natural flora and fauna by upsetting the ecological balance of the river and radically changing the level of the subterranean water.

(iii) For the same reason the agriculture and fishing of the region — the economic prerequisite of the local population — will also suffer serious losses.

(iv) The GNBS will result in the disappearance or dramatic transformation of a historic and natural landscape and ruin valuable archeological remains — these last two points would mean particularly serious losses for the Hungarians, since the region has played a special role in Hungarian history. Today it has considerable tourist value.

(v) Geological and seismological considerations have been neglected in the plans, although huge reservoirs often cause earthquakes.

(vi) Flood control could be solved by cheaper and safer means and, above all, in the case of an accident the flooding engendered would be more extensive than in the past; yet no measures have been taken to prevent such an incident or protect the surroundings.

(vii) Navigation conditions could be improved by much cheaper and simpler means if Soviet shipping interests were not exclusively dominant. (There is also a Slovakian–Hungarian conflict of interest here, since the construction of the GNBS would make Bratislava a big international port, taking over the present role of the Csepel Free Port in Budapest.

(viii) The scheme fits into an obsolete concept emphasizing the production of energy instead of more efficient use of it: in the framework of the latter consideration the energy produced by the GNBS would not be needed.

(ix) The amount of energy produced is insignificant when compared to the enormous ecological harm it causes — and especially insignificant for Hungary, which will have to hand over two-thirds of its share in the produced energy to amortize its debts to Austria within 20 years and a further amount to Czechoslovakia, since the latter country also contributed to the construction of the Hungarian part of the scheme.

(x) From an economic point of view the project will incur huge losses, even in the long run. All its stated benefits could have been realized by safer and cheaper means, without raising credits, without diverting resources from more important goals and without ruining other — more valuable — resources.

(xi)   The project is in conflict with Hungarian national interests.

According to the cost–benefit analysis of an expert committee (Hardi et al., 1989), the complete cancellation of the project would be more favorable in the long run from an economic point of view, and for the Hungarians, even in the short run the costs of cancellation and continuation would be about the same. The Hardi Report suggests that a solution could also be found for the international legal aspects: compensation agreement or litigation between Austria and Hungary. At the same time modification of the Czechoslovak–Hungarian agreement could be initiated with reference to the points that stipulate the preservation of water quality and other environmental guarantees which have not yet been implemented, and a bilateral agreement could be reached in terms of the net difference of gains and losses caused to both sides by the abandonment of the project.

5. The international conflict

Czechoslovakia unilaterally commended the construction work in April 1978, two months before the agreement was ratified by the Federal Parliament. The Hungarians were less enthusiastic: shortly after work began on the Hungarian side, in May 1980, the Hungarian Hydrological Association and the Patriotic People's Front organized a debate in which biologists and engineers sharply criticized the project. Czechoslovakia reacted by speeding up construction. In November 1981, János Vargha, a leading Hungarian environmental protester, published a highly critical article on the project (Vargha, 1981). The Slovak press resented the publication of the article in Hungary and referred to the 2,700 million Czech crowns already spent by Czechoslovakia on the project (*új Szó*, Bratislava, February 12, 1982).

In the early 1980s, Hungary experienced the first waves of its deepening economic crisis, therefore the government ordered a review of major national investments and suspended credits for the GNBS: its construction came to a virtual standstill. The government unilaterally postponed all work until 1990 and initiated a study on the ecological consequences of the dam system. The water management lobby sought to influence the results of the investigations in accordance with its interests; expert committees were formed again and again, but their findings were distorted by the lobby.

The Hungarian state and party leaders who were more concerned about the lack of long-term investment capital than about the ecological consequences, proposed that Czechoslovakia should build the whole project without Hungarian participation, while in exchange Hungary would pay off half the investment costs with electric energy. They made a similar proposal to Austria: if Austria participated in the construction of the Nagymaros plant, Hungary would pay for the work done with electric energy. Chancellor Sinowatz and the Hungarian government began to negotiate the transaction in November 1983.

In the meantime bilateral negotiations with Czechoslovakia yielded very poor results for the Hungarians: they were given only four years' respite and the Czechoslovakian side was prepared to take over only some of the work. In October 1983, the results of the negotiations were confirmed by the signing of a protocol. The summit meeting between Kádár and Husák in November 1983 was a further sign of confirmation and the agreement was ratified by the Czechoslovak Parliament in the same year. The Hungarian Parliament ratified it in 1984 (Kien, 1984).

Uncertainty at the highest level concerning the project proved to be fertile ground for public debate and controversy in Hungary. However, these debates and arguments could have no effect during the years of postponement, since the decision had already been made in June 1983 when the Politburo discussed the subject and secretly decided that the project was to be completed. It explains why that the government had no other alternative in August 1985 than re-committing itself to the scheme.

In the meantime, negotiations between Hungary and Austria for a credit agreement were under way. The Hungarian government would not have been able to continue construction without finding a solution to its financial problems. The solution came from Austria, where the construction of the Hainburg hydroelectric plant had been stopped by popular protest. Donaukraftwerke, (DOKW) the Austrian firm which would have constructed the Hainburg project, was happy to make a contract with the Hungarians to build a similar plant in Hungary. The agreement between Austria and Hungary was signed in May 1986: 70% of the Hungarian work was to be given to an Austrian contractor (DOKW), and the investment was to be paid with Austrian credit. Hungary was to pay off these credits by supplying electricity to Austria, starting in 1996. The intention was to produce 3,775 gigawatt hours per year, divided equally between Czechoslovakia and Hungary. Two-thirds of Hungary's share was to be paid to Austria over a period of 20 years, mainly during the winter months. Since the level and the flow of the Danube is at its lowest during the winter, new power stations would need to be built in Hungary to amortize the energy debt.

After the Hungarian government had decided to continue the

project, the growing criticism of scientists and environmentalists was suppressed and published materials about GNBS were censored. Work began at Nagymaros in 1987. However, parallel to the slow blossoming of Hungarian democracy, especially after Kádár's removal in 1988, freedom of speech became less and less restricted. A small number of independent politicians and even some representatives of the opposition succeeded in becoming elected to the Hungarian Parliament at the 1985 elections. In fact, this was the first time that more than one candidate had been allowed to run for one seat in the Parliament. Some of these newcomers initiated the re-examination of the project in the summer of 1988. The proposed debate in Parliament took place in October 1988, but the MPs—under strong pressure from the government and the party leadership—voted for the continuation of the project.

This decision was followed by an even more heated public debate and political struggle—also within the party leadership. The reformist wing of the party was gradually gaining ground, and in November 1988, Miklós Németh, a prominent reformist, became Prime Minister. The party reformers needed popular support in their fight against the conservative wing of the party (and were therefore more receptive to the claims of public opinion and the opposition) and mainly used the GNBS case as a political tool in their struggle.

However, the new Prime Minister sent a delegation to Czechoslovakia in February 1989 to sign a protocol concerning the speeding up of the work. But then three months later—in May 1989—his government unilaterally suspended work at Nagymaros for two months. By then, the reformists had become stronger: they publicly admitted that the 1956 Hungarian uprising was not a 'counter-revolution'—as it had earlier been labelled by the party—and the people killed in it were ceremonially re-buried one month later, in June 1989.

The government asked the Parliament to authorize a new round of negotiations with Czechoslovakia on a modification of the 1977 bilateral agreement and to commission expert bodies which would examine the consequences and possible decision alternatives. In June, the Parliament—the same MPs who had voted for continuation in October—approved the government's proposal. In July, Németh announced the suspension of all work at the upper dam in Dunakiliti as well.

The still conservative communist Czechoslovakia reacted with crushing words: its press accused the Hungarian government of submitting to political pressure by the opposition and labelled the decision anti-socialist and hostile to Czechoslovakia, jeopardizing the 'good neighborly' relations of the two countries. The Slovak leadership demanded completion of the project in its original form, otherwise it would file a claim for compensation of at least 2,700 million Czech crowns.

The Austrian government declared that it would respect the Hungarian government's decision, but it also had to defend the interests of the Austrian contractors: it hoped to reach an agreement with Hungary on due compensation.

In order to reduce the conflict with Czechoslovakia, in July Németh had a meeting with Adamec, Prime Minister of Czechoslovakia, and explained the Hungarian position to him. They decided to nominate a joint expert committee to examine the case thoroughly and to discuss the disputed facts and arguments. Adamec promised that if the committee found new facts or changes of circumstances after the agreement was signed, Czechoslovakia would accept the Hungarian point of view. They also agreed to extend the suspension period until the end of October, when they would make the final decision together.

The joint expert committees started to work but their discussions were not fruitful. The Czechoslovakian experts accused the Hungarians of not having produced any new facts after 1977 that could justify a modification of the original contract. The case strained the already tense relations between the two countries—resulting from the growing difference between their political systems—even further. Czechoslovakia demanded a huge sum in compensation, saying that the Hungarians had violated the inter-state contract. Hungary rejected the Czechoslovakian demands, arguing that all the benefits and expenses, damage and risks, as well as the costs of preventing damage and reducing risks, must be equally shared between the two countries as had originally been agreed.

In September, Czechoslovakia threatened to continue construction alone if the Hungarians withdrew from the project. Czechoslovakian politicians and experts spoke of 'new technical solutions' which would make the unilateral diversion of the Danube possible: thus they would not need the reservoir at Dunakiliti for filling up the weir at Körtvélyes and starting the turbines at Gabcikovo. At this point the tension between the two countries reached its climax. The Hungarians suspected that Czechoslovakia was only bluffing, trying to put pressure on the Hungarian decision-makers by blackmailing them. Still, there was no certainty about this either.

After an unsuccessful attempt to negotiate the matter with the other party, the Hungarians likewise resorted to threats, saying that a unilateral diversion of the Danube by Czechoslovakia would entail a unilateral modification of the common border, which would violate the peace treaties of 1946 and 1920. Thus bilateral affairs would be turned into an international issue. At the end of October the Hungarian Parliament approved the government's report on the investigations of expert bodies into the economic, ecological and technical aspects of the project and authorized the government to initiate a modification of the 1977 inter-state agreement. The Hungarian Parliament requested the government to act on the basis of ecological considerations and the priority of national interests.

In this desperate state of stalemate the Hungarian government proposed a compromise to Czechoslovakia. This compromise was greatly resented by the Hungarian environmental movement, because —in exchange for the abandonment of the Nagymaros part of the project—it would have allowed Czechoslovakia to complete and use the Gabcikovo dam provided it gave appropriate ecological guarantees. According to the environmentalists such guarantees simply did not exist. Czechoslovakia was ready to give these guarantees if the Gabcikovo part of the project could be built in accordance with the original plans.

In the autumn of 1989, radical political changes in Czechoslovakia gave the Hungarians high hopes for a solution to the conflict. In January 1990, therefore, Hungary made a new proposal: instead of employing the compromise which had been proposed by Hungary under pressure in November 1989 as a starting point, the conflict should be solved by the two governments on the basis of the results of scientific investigations to be made by independent experts and inter-national insitutions. The Hungarian environmental organizations demanded that no work should be carried out on the site, except maintenance, until free elections had been held in both countries.

The new Czechoslovakian leadership used a dramatically different tone from that of its predecessor. The new attitude—especially rep-resented by Vaclav Havel, the new President of Czechoslovakia—was neither suspicious, nor reserved but much friendlier towards Hungary. Czechoslovakian environmentalist movements were no longer denied the freedom of the press, nor their activities prohibited—they could activate/mobilize public opinion. The new government desisted from the unilateral diversion of the Danube and agreed to set up expert committees to investigate the ecological and economic aspects of the project. In February, Wladimir Lokvenc, a Slovakian commissary of the investment, who had fanatically defended the scheme for decades, was dismissed by the Slovakian government.

These were positive steps, but the Hungarians were still not fully satisfied as to the behavior of the new Czechoslovakian government. Although it was more receptive to ecological concerns than the previous government and readily admitted that the idea of the whole investment had been a mistake, it still insisted on completing construction because of the huge sums of money already invested and because the Slovakian contribution to the construction was lacking only one-tenth of the total. According to Slovakian decision-makers, the hydroelectric plant at Gabcikovo, after having acquired the necessary secondary installations to protect the environment, ought to produce energy in order to amortize the investment costs. However, they were prepared to accept the less risky, continuous mode of operation, instead of the originally planned peak-time energy generation, which is more disastrous to the environment. Hardliners, who even wanted to put the question of Nagymaros and peak-time energy generation back on the agenda, started to re-gain influence in the Slovak government. Supporters and opponents of the project were fighting each other.

The first free elections took place in the early spring of 1990 in Hungary and in early summer in Czechoslovakia. In Hungary a mid-right coalition led by the Hungarian Democratic Forum formed the government. Its policy on the GNBS is similar to that of the Németh government. In Czechoslovakia the civil forum won the elections; but, unfortunately, this did not result in a radical shift of Czechoslovak GNBS policy. One reason for this is that several members of the previous communist government joined the victorious Civil Forum and were appointed to high positions in the new government (including top positions in the environment and energy administrations), while their real views did not change much. On the other hand, ex-opposition politicians ceased to criticize the GNBS scheme once they took on 'the burden and responsibilities of power'. A more important reason is that those opposed to the project have had less time (compared to Hungary) to convince decision-makers and the public. At the same time national sentiments have been not against, as in Hungary, but for the project— thus it could not become a symbol of the struggle between totalitarianism and democracy. The third reason is that the federal government— which has more than enough trouble with Slovak separatists—does not want to interfere with a Slovak national cause and does not mind if Slovak nationalism is directed against Hungarians instead of the Czechs. Thus the advent of democracy has not swept away the Gabcikovo part of the project and has not brought an end to the Czechoslovak–Hungarian dispute. Neither has Hungary's conflict with Austria yet been resolved.

Last year the Austrian claim for compensation was about 2,000 million Austrian schillings in addition to the bill of 850 million for the work already done by the Austrian contractor. In May 1989, after the Hungarian government suspended construction, a goodwill delegation of Hungarian MPs and environmentalists travelled to Vienna to ask the Austrians not to demand too much compensation from the Hungarian government, because this would cause further economic difficulties for Hungary. They also sought to convince their partners of the importance of preserving the natural values of the Danube and the area around it. The delegation met the representatives of four parliamentary parties, Donaukraftwerke, the Verbundgesellschaft, the Länder Bank, the Kreditanstalt, and the Austrian green movements. The Austrian Freiheitspartei and the Green Party showed sympathy for the Hungarian standpoint and emphasized that the recovery of the Hungarian economy is of long-term interest to Austria. The Greens were of the opinion that the Austrian contractors should limit their claims to the costs of work already performed and should renounce any further compensation; Austria should not stick to the energy transport contract, because it will force the Hungarians to build a new power station. However, the discussion between the delegation and the representatives of Donaukraftwerke ended in mutual disappointment.

In July 1989 the Austrian economic minister declared that the Austrian contractors would claim 'only' 2,600 million schillings, provided Hungary would pay the sum immediately in cash. Otherwise— for example, if Hungary amortized its debts by supplying energy—this sum would be increased by interest due. The minister rejected the Hungarian proposal that the Austrian firms could be compensated by new contracts (e.g. road-building) in Hungary. The Hungarians considered the claim for interest unfair, since Hungary did not denounce the energy supply treaty.

In May 1990 Donaukraftwerke made its claim officially: 3,850 million schillings plus 250–300 million schillings as interest. According to DOKW the cost of work already done was 950 million, and the rest consisted of materials already ordered, the cost of preparatory work, unrealized profits, etc. This sum would be amortized by supplying electricity. Debates over the cogency of this huge compensation claim can last for months, even years.

6. The domestic conflicts

6.1 In Czechoslovakia

Public and expert opinion had the least immediate impact on decision-making in Czechoslovakia. Although there has been some debate over the GNBS also within the Czechoslovak administration, these debates were successfully concealed. Concern over the project had barely been tolerated in the previous regime: public discussion had been suppressed and no arguments against the scheme had been permitted in the media; at the same time there had been a steady flow of propaganda in the media in favor of the project and against the protesters.

The first professionally valid—although not comprehensive—criticism came in 1976 from two institutes of the Slovak Academy of Sciences. In 1988 the Ecological Section of the Academy produced the first full critique of the scheme, which was then published in January 1989.

While opposition in the Czech Republic was not tolerated, in Slovakia criticism within registered organizations could be more extensive. The most active opposition has come from the Bratislava city branch of the Slovak Union of Nature and Landscape Protectors (SZOPK), which has been criticizing the project for 10 years. SZOPK published its first proclamation on the GNBS in its magazine in 1981. Soon after that, however, the magazine was suppressed for six months, and then all censorship was tightened up. Nevertheless, in 1988 the magazine was able to devote a whole issue to the case without penalties (Fisher, 1989). In 1979 SZOPK published a proposal for a 'Danube River Landscape National Park', this being extended in 1988 to the idea of an International Park. Hungarian and Austrian environmentalists endorsed the Danube Proclamation (which was the only open joint Czech–Slovak venture), including the proposal for the International Park.

In the Czech Republic opposition could only appear underground, for example in the framework of Charter 77, and criticism could only be published in samizdat. In May 1989, an individual wrote an open letter to Federal Prime Minister Adamec, calling for changes to the Gabcikovo system and a stop to construction at Nagymaros. The letter had collected over 3,600 signatures, many times more than any other such petition. It was followed by an increased administrative harassment (arrests, confiscation of passports, etc.) of the unofficial environmentalist circles (Fischer, 1989).

After the democratic revolution of December 1989, harassment of environmentalists came to an end, and since then they have enjoyed an official status with legal possibilities to publish and mobilize.

6.2 In Hungary

In Hungary, professional debates developed in 1979–83. Some departments within the state administration (especially the energy sector) opposed the scheme on economic grounds. Such battles were kept within the administration, but secrecy was not preserved. Still, debates were confined to professional circles, and the public were not involved until 1981 when J. Vargha published a critical article (mentioned in Section 5) in a public periodical. Since 1981 committees and groups of scientists have prepared professional reports on the harmful effects of the project. In 1983 the presidium of the Hungarian Academy of Sciences condemned the plan in a classified report.

In the early 1980s the Hungarian government commissioned the National Office for Environmental Protection and Nature Conservation to prepare an environmental assessment of the GNBS. During the time of the study construction was suspended, due to financial problems. By the time the study was completed, the top party leadership had already decided to continue the project. The failure of the report, published in 1984, to approve the GNBS, led only to its being regarded as confidential and ignored (Fischer, 1989). Another consequence of the report was the dismissal of the director and the disbanding of the office in the following year.

By 1984, the debate spread from the limited circle of professionals to the public. Various official organizations and institutions organized lectures and public debates on the GNBS. In February 1984 János Vargha delivered a lecture—which was followed by a heated debate—on the dam system, which in fact launched the first unofficial environmental movement in Eastern Europe: the 'Committee for the Danube'. (Its aim was to inform the public by organizing lectures and distributing leaflets, but it also collected signatures against the dam system, organized marches and was lobbying MPs).

The movement grew in size but it was not structured, and it became chaotic. It was therefore sought—unsuccessfully—to found an official association. The political leadership became frightened of the growing sympathy for the movement and toughened its position, prohibiting public discussion and publications against the GNBS. Finding itself unable to organize an association, the movement therefore formed the unofficial Danube Circle (which became a registered organization only in 1988) (Sólyom, 1988).

The refusal of official registration limited the number of participants in the movement, which therefore could not present itself as an organization with a membership; it had no political program or political tactics. Generally, ecological movements in Hungary were case-oriented, and no national network of the separate movements around a common ideological platform was organized (Szabó, 1988).

The Danube Circle broke the ban on public discussion of the GNBS by publishing the 'News of the Danube Circle' in samizdat. The bulletin contained documents of debates, information on the historical and political background of the project and an account of the debate in Austria on the Hainburg hydroelectric plant. In December 1985 the Danube Circle received the Right Livelihood Award (the 'Alternative Nobel Prize'). It wished to use the prize money for scientific research into the ecology of the Danube region by creating an endowment for this purpose, but it proved impossible to realize this under the political conditions of the time. This, again, caused a crisis in the movement.

While the Danube Circle was paralyzed, three other movements appeared for a short period: one gathered signatures, demanding a referendum; the 'Blues' demanded that Parliament should discuss the case and decide on it; the 'Friends of the Danube' demanded that at least the construction of the dam at Nagymaros should be stopped.

In 1986 the Danube Circle concentrated first of all on the fight against Austrian involvement in construction work. (It had already protested against the Austrian participation in 1984.) In January 1986 the Danube Circle, together with the Austrian and German Greens, held a press conference, protesting against the Austrian financing of the GNBS. The Danube Circle also sent a petition to the Austrian Parliament. In February a 'Danube Walk' was organized by the Danube Circle and the Austrian Greens, which was violently disrupted by the Hungarian police. The government's action was internationally condemned and the European Parliament passed a protest resolution (Fischer, 1989). In April 30 prominent Hungarian intellectuals published a full-page advertisement in an Austrian daily, *Die Presse*, asking the Austrians to protest against their government's involvement in the GNBS. In May 1988 there was a demonstration against Austria's role in the case in front of the Austrian embassy in Budapest.

Starting from 1988, the political climate in Hungary changed and opposition was revitalized. Because the work at Gabcikovo was already advanced, attention was focused on Nagymaros and peak-time production of electricity. In August 1988, 15 environmental groups came together in the Nagymaros Action Committee, financed by the WWF. In September 1988 a two-day international conference was organized by the WWF and the Danube Circle. Among the participants there were some Austrian Greens, the Austrian Minister for the Environment, representatives from the Hungarian Academy of Sciences, from the International Rivers Network, and from the Hungarian Union of Young Democrats (Fisher, 1989).

There were further demonstrations and petitions before the October 1988 sitting of the Hungarian Parliament, where 32 MPs tabled a resolution requesting a referendum. The Communist Party treated voting as a loyalty test: it obliged its members in Parliament to reject the referendum. The formation of a parliamentary party fraction in a one-party system raised serious questions as to the legitimacy of the Parliament and also the possibility of keeping the one-party system at all. This was one of the first parliamentary sessions televised from beginning to end, and masses of voters could thus witness the manipulations in Parliament and could follow the activity of their representatives. After the parliamentary debate and voting, voters and the opposition in several constituencies started to collect signatures to call back those representatives who had spoken in favor and had voted for the continuation of construction at Nagymaros. This became a campaign to get rid of orthodox communist MPs. After the Parliament's decision the Danube Circle collected some 120,000 signatures, demanding a referendum.

To sum up: this case played an important role in the Hungarian democratization process. The GNBS investment became a symbol of the old regime, against which all opposition forces were fighting, together with the reformist wing of the Communist Party. Soon after the reformist wing of the party came to power, political freedom was rapidly introduced, including a free press and a multi-party system. After May 1989 the referendum was no longer needed: the new government suspended construction.

Now the focus of attention of the opponents turned to the battle against the water-management bureaucracy, who—under the guise of maintenance work—did everything in order to continue construction (and, of course, the Slovakian party did not stop either), thus raising the bill to be paid to the Austrian contractors. The next battle had to be won at the (Fall) session of Parliament, when MPs would make a final decision on the fate of the project. In the meantime, committees of scientists made investigations into possible alternatives, their costs and benefits. Among these committees was one of independent experts from the WWF, Hungary, Austria, Czechoslovakia and some other countries (Hardi et al., 1989). The battle was won with the parliamentary decision to abandon the Nagymaros part of the project.

In April 1990 János Vargha won the Goldman prize, founded for rewarding prominent protectors of the environment, and established an institute for East European environmental research.

6.3 In Austria

There was also a political fight over the GNBS in Austria because the government committed itself to back the Austrian contractor firms. In addition, the Austrian government has had difficulties with power stations, being unable to start an already completed nuclear power station at Zwentendorf 12 years ago because of public protests and a referendum rejecting its starting up. Plans to build a hydroelectric plant at Hainburg on the Danube had to be abandoned for the same reason in 1984, and a plan to jointly construct a hydroelectric plant with Czechoslovakia at Wolfsthal could likewise not be realized. The GNBS seemed to be very good business: Austria could import very cheap electricity and at the same time guarantee employment to construction workers and firms. But the Austrian Greens protested again, sending petitions to Austrian MPs in 1986, and MPs of the Green Party were protesting to the Austrian government. Some MPs from the Green Party distributed leaflets in Budapest against a visit to Nagymaros by Austrian officials, this leading to several detentions and expulsions (Fisher, 1989). Other environmental groups also protested against the government's role in the GNBS project: in 1986 the Konrad Lorenz group proposed the suspension of construction pending assessments on environmental impact; the Global 2000 group occupied the building of the management of Donaukraftwerke in 1988 as a sign of protest.

Some representatives of the Austrian People's Party (ÖVP, which was in coalition with the Socialist Party) used the case as a tool in their political fight with the SPÖ. Erhard Busek, president of the Vienna organization of the ÖVP, compared the behavior of the big Austrian companies to that of the Hungarian government.

Now that the Nagymaros construction has been discontinued and the contracts between Austria and Hungary have lost their validity, the fight is going on over the amount of compensation. The Austrian Greens have tried to put pressure on the government not to support the high sums sought by the contractors: only the price of work already carried out should be claimed. However, they have little chance of winning.

7. Conclusions

The GNBS case is an exceptionally interesting environmental conflict to analyze because the three countries involved have been so different politically during the period examined. Austria represents a Western democracy, while Czechoslovakia and Hungary were communist countries at the beginning of the story, and both became pluralist democracies by the end. But the pace of democratization was very different in the two countries: in Hungary it was gradual, dating back to 1985 and speeding up only after 1987, while in Czechoslovakia the change was sudden and radical, like an explosion, in December 1989.

Comparing the behavior of the three countries in the conflict leads us
to interesting observations.

(a) The conflict has had similar elements in all three countries,
regardless of political system: the main conflict is between civil society
and groups having economic and political power.

In Czechoslovakia the most enthusiastic supporter of the project has
been the Slovak government, enjoying the backing of the federal
government. The Slovak water-management bureaucracy, their engineers and experts, companies taking part in construction, politicians,
and the apparatus of the Communist Party were also on the supporters' side. In Hungary the same kind of groups were committed to
the project, with a difference only on the political level: the project
never enjoyed the unanimous approval of the whole party and government leadership, and the bureaucracy was also divided. To a certain
extent workers employed on the construction, together with their labor
union representatives, were also among the supporters in both
countries. In Austria the supporter side consisted of the contracting
firms, the Austrian government, representatives of the coalition parties in power (especially the Austrian Socialist Party) and the labor
union defending the employment of the Austrian construction
workers.

On the opposing side we find the environmental movements, concerned scientists and other representatives of the civic communities of
the three countries. The political opposition supported them in all
three countries, but more on the basis of political than on environmental considerations (like the ÖVP in Austria, or the Civil Forum in
Czechoslovakia, which, after coming to power, 'modified' its approach
to the Gabcikovo plant). In Hungary the whole opposition made use of
the case in its fight against the political system; even the reformist
communists used it as a tool in their political fight against the more
orthodox old leadership.

What is of great interest is to observe signs of transnational cooperation among both the opponents and the supporter forces of the
three countries, and a similarity of the structure of the domestic
conflicts, regardless of political systems.

(b) None the less, the political system of each country did matter.
Although we can find economic short-sightedness and ecologically
disastrous projects in all political systems, in the non-market economies of the communist regimes there have been fewer limits to ruining
the environment, because even economic rationality has been over-
ruled by ideological considerations. Moreover, in a non-democratic
political system decisions are made by a small group of people without
any social control. The same group also monopolize information.

Society at large has no chance of taking part in the decision-making process, judging the alternatives or even knowing about them. Citizens are often informed about a decision only after it has been made—if they are informed at all. The possibilities for them to criticize the decisions of the political leadership, to organize themselves in order to express and defend their interests, and their freedom of speech, are very limited or non-existent. Their efforts to express views different to the official standpoint are regarded as hostile and politically danger-ous even in the case of non-political subjects. In such systems all issues and controversies tend to become challenges to the legitimacy of the system. Therefore it is easy to commit mistakes, but extremely diffi-cult to correct them.

Environmental protest has thus played an important role in the democratization process in the so-called socialist countries: in order to be able to defend effectively the citizens' rights to a healthy environ-ment, environmentalists have been forced to fight for freedom of speech, freedom of association, a free press, political pluralism and democracy.

(c) Nevertheless, democracy is not a panacea for environmental problems. In parliamentary democracies interests are represented through political parties, but for most of them—except perhaps for the Greens—other considerations are often more important than the en-vironmental ones. If they support (or give in to) an environmental cause, they do so mainly for political considerations. The behaviour of the Austrian government in the GNBS case is very illustrative of this: while it was forced to retreat in face of the citizens' protest in the case of ecologically risky projects on Austrian territory, it did not hesitate to finance and support a similar project in a country where the citizens' rights were suppressed. Austria behaved in a neo-colonialist way, mak-ing use of the economic hardship and oppressive regime of its poorer neighbor (Konrád, 1987; Schonesberger, 1987).

Although Hungary and Czechoslovakia have acquired democratic political systems, the danger is still there of their becoming 'environ-mental colonies' of the richer Western countries (this is true of all the East European countries) because they desperately need Western investment and are economically dependent on the West. Further-more, changing their economic systems will take a long time. With the restructuring of their economy they face a new wave of industrializa-tion, and it will be extremely difficult for countries in deep economic crisis to give priority to the environment over the allure of money. To prevent this, a well-organized environmental movement and high ecological awareness of the population are needed.

(d) The fact that this conflict, basically domestic in all three countries, became one between them can be explained by a combination of the different levels of their commitments to the project (according to their expected gains and losses) and their different sensitivity to domestic pressure. Hungary has been the least committed because it has had the most to lose through the project, which rather served Slovak and Soviet than Hungarian interests. Slovakia has also had a lot to lose, but it has regarded the expected gains as outweighing this: the scheme has suited age-old Slovak national aspirations, so that from a nationalistic point of view Slovakia could only gain from the project. (In this respect it has been a zero-sum game between Hungary and Czechoslovakia.) Austria had almost only gains to expect, while the risks would mainly appear in another country: this is why the Austrian government was less sensitive to any pressure from the environmental movements.

In Czechoslovakia the system was so oppressive that the opponents of the scheme could have no serious impact on decision-makers. Hungary in the late 1980s was in the phase of political transition to a democratic system, and was therefore even more sensitive to political pressure than the already established democracies (especially because the reformist communists recognized the usefulness of the case in their political fight for power). The difference in pace between the political processes of the two socialist countries added an extra dimension to the conflict: the more and more open environmental and political protest in Hungary endangered not only the completion of the GNBS scheme, but also the regime itself. The activity of the Hungarian environmental movements encouraged corresponding movements in Slovakia. The Czechoslovakian party leaders were afraid of the power of example—and they were right. The example of other countries became an important factor in the democratic revolution in Eastern Europe. Since real conflict between civil society and the central leadership could not evolve in Czechoslovakia due to repressive measures, the conflict appeared as an international one: it seemed as if menace to the regime came from outside, not from within. Today, when both countries have democratic systems, one obstacle in the way of solving the conflict has disappeared, while others, e.g. different national interests, different levels of commitment, still remain.

Note

This chapter was written more than a year ago. A lot of new developments could have been added to the narrative, but the analysis still seems to be valid. The Slovak government has shown some willingness for compromise by developing several alternatives, ranging from the so-called 'zero-solution' (no dam, no power stations) to realization of the original plans (including Nagymaros); however, it is a tough negotiator and seems to be determined to complete and operate the Gabcikovo power station. It is still blackmailing the Hungarians by a unilateral solution (diverting the Danube) in case they do not compromise.

However, some more encouraging negotiations are going on behind the scenes, and most encouraging of all, popular protest and organized resistance against the dam are growing in Slovakia, thanks to the democratization processes in the country. Political developments in Slovakia seem to follow the Hungarian pattern of two years ago. These developments reinforce the conclusion of our paper: the interests and behavior of the 'players' in the conflict do not depend on the political system too much. The real difference is in the extent they are able to enforce their will and interests. Hopefully a more and more self-confident civil society in Slovakia will be able to force its government and water management lobby to give up a project threatening ecological disaster.

References

Borsos, B., 1989. 'Dams and reforms in the East'. Budapest. Manuscript.

Fisher, D., 1989. 'Public intervention in pollution aspects of transboundary watercourses and international lakes. European experience.' Manuscript.

Hardi, P. et al., 1989. 'The Hardi Report. Summary for the Council of Ministers of an expert review concerning the ecological, environmental, technical, economic, international and legal issues of the Bös-Nagymaros Barrage System'. Budapest.

Hildyard, N. and Goldsmith, E., 1984. *The Social and Environmental Effects of Large Dams*, Volume I. (Volume II: 1986). Wadebridge Ecological Centre, Cornwall.

Kien, P. (pseudonym of János Vargha), 1984. 'A Nagy Szlovák Csatorna', *Beszélö*, no. 9, samizdat.

Konrád, Gy., 1987. 'A barátság feltétele', in M. Köcher (ed.), *Nagymaros*. Edition öH−Verlag der österreichischen Hochschülerschaft, Grüne Bildungswerkstatt: Vienna.

Schonesberger, G., 1987. 'Uns bleibt die Schande', in M. Köcher (ed.), *Nagymaros*. Edition öH−Verlag der österreichischen Hochschülerschaft, Grüne Bildungswerkstatt: Vienna.

Sólyom, L., 1988. 'A társadalom részvétele a környezetvédelemben', in L. Sólyom and M. Szabó (eds), *A zöld hullám*. Eötvös Loránd Turományegyetem állam- es Jogtudományi Kar: Budapest.

Szabó, M., 1988. 'Vannak-e alternativ társadalmi mozgalmak Magyarországon?', in L. Sólyom and M. Szabó (eds), *A zöld hullám*. Eötvös Lóránd Tudómáneygyetem állam- és Jogtudományi Kar: Budapest.

Vargha, J., 1981. 'Egyre távolabb ajótól', *Valóság*, 1981, no. 11.

7 Land Tenure and Environmental Conflict: The Case of the Inland Niger Delta, Mali[1]

Richard Moorehead

1. Introduction

This chapter presents data and an argument researched between 1981 and 1988 in the inland delta of the river Niger in Mali. Its theme is that even if environmental change is the immediate motivator behind the endemic violence surrounding access to resources in the delta, the context and possibility of it arising is closely linked to changes that have taken place in the *land tenure system* since the turn of the century. These changes are strongly related to events that took place in the colonial era, which significantly shaped the manner in which present land tenure policy is put into practice today. This, in turn, does much to define, during a period of drought, where, when and how environmental conflict takes place in the delta now.

It is often overlooked that rural populations living in drought-prone areas have evolved sophisticated strategies to cope with environmental risk, and that they experience if not drought then difficult periods several times in each generation. These coping strategies include savings mechanisms whereby rural producers accumulate stocks to take them through difficult years, sharing mechanisms between wealthy and poor, and, most importantly, transhumant cycles to gain access to different ecosystems in times of environmental stress, when their own system is not sufficiently productive.

Crucial to this latter strategy is a land tenure system which allows rural producers reciprocal access to resources both within and between ecosystems. In the inland Niger delta this relied in the past upon relations of kinship and consanguinity to provide a system for the management of the natural resources the community depended upon. Kinship relationships equally provided the basis for the exclusion of outside producers, reinforced by a system of beliefs which held that the traditional owners of resources had supernatural links with the spirits of the zone they inhabited.

In the last century these traditional land tenure systems were subjected to the theocratic state that administered the whole delta: while some redistribution of resources took place at that time, the management regimes governing access to natural resources remained substantially intact. In this century the colonial and post-colonial states have effectively penetrated all traditional management regimes found in the delta, undermining their ability on the one hand to allocate resources between members of their community, and on the other to exclude outsiders. In many cases the response of local producers has been violent.

Over the last 15 years the productivity of the inland Niger delta has fallen considerably. In common with other parts of the Sahel, the rural population has responded by moving—some out of the area altogether, but others, more significantly, to deeper parts of the delta where productivity is highest. The arrival of large numbers of competitors wishing to settle in these areas has provoked serious conflict between customary inhabitants and the outsiders. This conflict, directly linked to environmental stress, concerns three players: the post-colonial state, local inhabitants and newcomers. Outsiders, with superior access to funds and representatives in the state apparatus, are often able to establish a claim to resources they never had before being backed by the sanction of the present government. The Malian administration, in several ways, is overseeing the destruction of local management regimes which provide the basis for effective environmental conservation by the people most concerned: local inhabitants with traditional rights of ownership.

The chapter is divided into six brief parts. The first presents the physical characteristics of the zone, sketches the nature of the rural economy, and describes the onset of drought over the last 20 years. The two following sections set out the property systems of the past and their evolution to the present day, including a description of the manner in which their destruction is providing future sources for conflict. In a further two sections the sort of environmental disputes found in the delta today are discussed, illustrated by reference to one set of conflicts over a fishery in the northern sector of the delta. In the conclusion an attempt is made to draw lessons from this local context for regional and national issues.

2. The delta

The inland Niger delta (see Figure 7.1) lies between 13°30' and 15°30'
latitude and 5°30' and 3°30' longitude in central Mali, West Africa. Its
chief characteristic is that it is a seasonally inundated floodplain with
a uniquely rich ecosystem on the southern reaches of the Sahara,
making it one of the most important wetlands, in terms of biodiversity
and in terms of productivity, in Africa.

This richness relies upon the coincidence between the flood regime
and rainfall in the region. The delta has four seasons: the rains, which
coincide with the arrival of the floodwaters, between June/July and
September; the high water season, when the area becomes an inland
sea covering up to 40,000 km^2, between October and December; the
falling water period between January and March, and the dry season,
when the zone takes on the aspect of a great dry plain, between April
and June. The delta lies between the 300 mm and 600 mm isohyets.

The dryland resources on the borders of the delta produce millet,
rainfed rice, sorghum, manioc, sweet potatoes, cotton and peanuts, as
well as forests, wild food and pasture; the wetlands of the delta proper
produce fish, floodland rice, wild food, pasture and floodland forest. The
area is renowned for the diversity of plant and animal life it sustains,
including 130 species of fish, 350 species of bird as well as numerous
large mammals, and for its productivity: floodland pasture has been
estimated at between 7,000–25,000 kg/ha of dry matter per year and
the fisheries have been reckoned to be able to produce 100,000 tons a
year (IUCN, 1989a).

The production of these resources is highly seasonal, and varies
considerably, year to year. Figure 7.2 summarises the timing and
period of exploitation of these resources through an 'average' year and
illustrates a fundamental principle as to when and where people make
use of their environment: while the delta is most inaccessible—when
the water is rising to its deepest level—production is concentrated on
the drylands, and when it is most accessible it is centred on the
floodplains themselves. This situation underlies the seasonal nature of
conflict in the delta, and aspects of the land tenure regimes found in
the area.

Dry years are hardly the exception in the inland Niger delta, and
drought is not uncommon: the Sahel has experienced seven in the last
century (ENDA, 1985). But beginning in 1982–3, and lasting until
1985–6, with further bad years in 1986–8, the area experienced the
lowest flood levels and rainfall since data began to be collected in the
early 1900s. The effect of low flood levels and rainfall on the delta has
been—in comparison to the 1960s—to increase the length of the dry

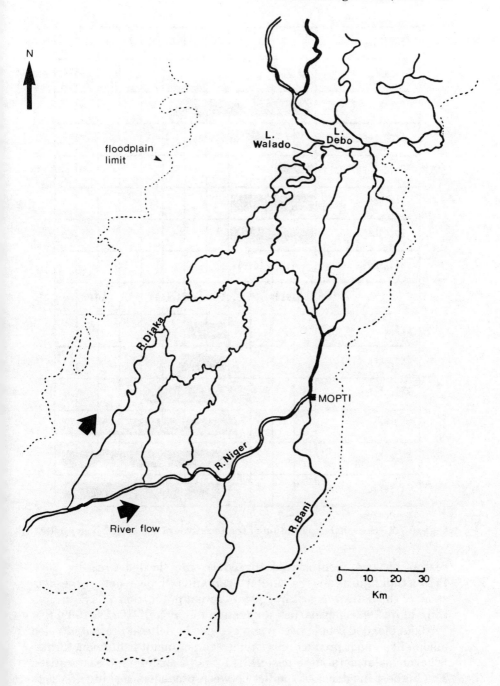

Figure 7.1   The inland delta of the river Niger

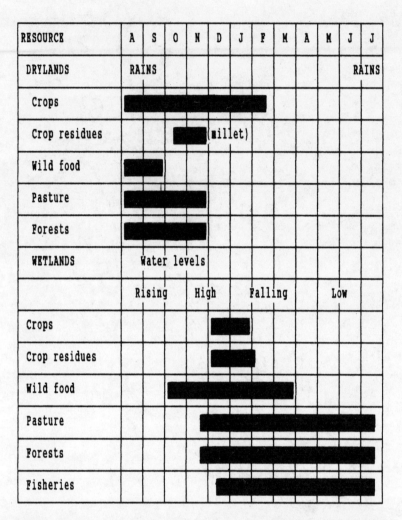

RESOURCE	A	S	O	N	D	J	F	M	A	M	J	J
DRYLANDS	RAINS											RAINS
Crops	████████████████████											
Crop residues			██	(millet)								
Wild food	██											
Pasture	██████											
Forests	██████											
WETLANDS	Water levels											
	Rising		High		Falling				Low			
Crops					████							
Crop residues					████							
Wild food			████████████									
Pasture				███████████████████								
Forests				███████████████████								
Fisheries					█████████████████████							

Figure 7.2 Seasonal exploitation of the resources of the inland Niger delta

season by two months and to reduce the flooded area by 75%. Production figures show a similar dramatic fall: over half of the livestock of the delta was lost in 1984–6, cereal production was down to a third of its 1960s' levels, fish production fell by half (IUCN, 1989b).

About 500,000 people live in and exploit the delta at present, divided among five major production systems: transhumant fishermen, farmer fishermen, farmers, agro-pastoralists and transhumant pastoralists. The highest incidence of conflict between producers seeking access to resources nowadays is firstly between transhumant fishermen and

farmer fishermen, and secondly between different groups of transhumant pastoralists. These two production systems depend more than
other groups on moving between ecological areas to gain their
livelihoods.

Transhumant fishermen—who also farm, but whose principal
activity is fishing—come from upstream parts of the delta. When the
waters begin to fall in October/November each year they leave their
villages (leaving behind the old, the young and the sick, and enough
people to see to the rice/millet harvest) and follow the course of the
Niger/Diaka rivers until they reach the Walado/Debo lake system at
the outset of the dry season. They remain there until the onset of the
rains, when they turn for home once more.

From when they leave their villages until the dry season they fish in
the territories of the farmer fishermen who live in deeper parts of the
delta and migrate less. This latter group grow flooded rice crops
between June/July and December before moving out to fishing camps
near their villages for the falling water season. In the dry season they
move back to their villages and fish the main waterways, using collective methods, often in the company of outsiders.

The transhumant pastoralists of the delta are made up of two
groups: those who are based in the drylands and who migrate into the
delta each year during the dry season, and those from the delta, who
own their own territories on the floodplains, and who migrate onto the
drylands each year when the delta is flooded.

The former group are made up of Tuareg, who raise camels, cattle
and smallstock in line with the drier conditions of the areas they come
from. They are regarded as strangers and often as traditional enemies
by delta Fulani, and traditionally both pay a tithe and are allowed onto
floodland pastures later than the owners of the floodplain grasslands.

The transhumant Fulani of the delta, at the onset of the rains, leave
the floodplains for the adjacent dryland pastures, moving, depending
on how good the rains are, several hundred kilometres away from the
delta. Customarily, as water points in the drylands shrink, they return
towards the delta floodplains and, through a set of complex crossing
points, follow the rich flood pastures as they are revealed by the
receding waters. By February/March they are on the dry lake beds in
the north of the zone, where they remain until the onset of the rains.
The Fulani specialise in cattle-raising in line with their preferential
access to dry season pasture in the delta. To give an idea of size, it is
estimated that over one million head of cattle and two million head of
sheep and goats use the floodplain each year—20% of the national herd
(RIM, 1987).

The effect of the drying out of the delta has been to raise the intensity of exploitation of the zone dramatically as the same number of people have been obliged to subsist on a narrower, and narrowing resource base. Transhumant fishermen who formerly returned to their home villages to fish and farm before moving downstream are nowadays installing themselves semi-permanently in the lake region; transhumant herders now keep their herds in the delta for longer periods of time and do not transhume as far as they used to in case the rains stop suddenly; farmer fishermen as well as transhumant fishermen are using more intensive fishing gear to catch their quarry; a cash market is developing for wild products that were rarely sold before (wild grains, dried pasture, wild fruit, waterfowl) and increasing exploitation is taking place for forest products (household fuel) that have been commercialised for some time. Growing levels of conflict, both within and between production systems, is accompanying this process.

At the same time customary systems of managing access to resources in the delta are being destroyed. Former rules linking fishing communities to traditional seasonal visitors, herding communities to reciprocal access rights with neighbouring herding areas, and the overall flexibility of a system which provided a safety net to indigenous inhabitants of the delta is fast breaking down. While this is being greatly accelerated by present environmental conditions, the roots of this process go back at least to the beginning of the last century, and are much influenced by factors other than the natural threat of drought.

3. Property systems in the past

The inland Niger delta, before the French colonial period (1893–1960), had two major land tenure systems, which governed access to all resources on both the floodplains and the neighbouring drylands.

The first and most ancient system was that which accorded the right of the first-comer to 'own' and control an area. Under this system communities were divided into founding lineages, lineages that arrived later and married into the founding lines (consanguine lineages) and later-arriving strangers. In addition to these three groups there were visitors who came customarily each year to exploit the communities' zone, and who paid a tithe for the right.

The head of this community was the resource manager—'master of the water' or a 'master of the land'—whose duties included the arbitration of disputes, setting the dates for the start and end of major productive activities through the year, and the authorisation of access to strangers wishing to exploit the area either seasonally or on a longer-term basis. These resource managers derived their authority in part from the supernatural relationship they had with the water and land spirits of the zone, and they were responsible for the sacrifices needed to propitiate these spiritual owners of resources.

The delta was divided in the past into a number of defined fishing and farming territories, and the original founding lineages and masters of the water/land were known to all inhabitants or seasonal visitors to the district. To this day in many parts of the delta there is a broad consensus as to who these original inhabitants were, and the powers of the 'master of the water' are still respected, if not feared, by many.

The second major land tenure system was imposed on the delta by the pastoralists (Fulani) who colonised the area in successive waves from the twelfth century to the nineteenth. In the eighteenth and nineteenth centuries the Fulani ruled the delta, firstly through secular, animist kingdoms on the floodplains and on its borders, then, between 1820–1862, as a unified theocratic state, known as the *dina* (Gallais, 1967).

Under the animist kingdoms the essential distinction was between the noble/free and slaves. The Fulani, divided into nomadic pastoral groups and more sedentary, village-based agro-pastoralists, installed slaves on the floodplains and the dry lands to cultivate for them and to form a standing army. These cultivators obtained access to land through force. Older fishing and farming communities in the area retained their independence under this system to the extent that they did not compete with the herding and cereal interests of the Fulani.

The *dina* system effectively incorporated the fishing and farming land tenure systems into a larger, regional administration that represented a primarily pastoral interest. The delta floodplains were divided into 30 or so pasturing territories, and a set of 'cantonnements' were created on the borderlands.

The cantonnements and pasturing territories—known as *leyde*—were managed generally by the heads of Fulani clans. Under the *dina* system there were three forms of pastoral property: that which belonged to the state, managed directly in its interest to provide revenue for administrative costs and to maintain a standing army; village pasture to provide feed for milk animals while the main herds were away on transhumance, and fields for slave cultivation of grains; in addition, there was collective pasture of the clan reserved for the use of transhumant herds. Fishing and farming resources belonging to indigenous peoples remained under independent management, though they paid a tithe.

Perhaps the most significant actions of the *dina* state were to codify

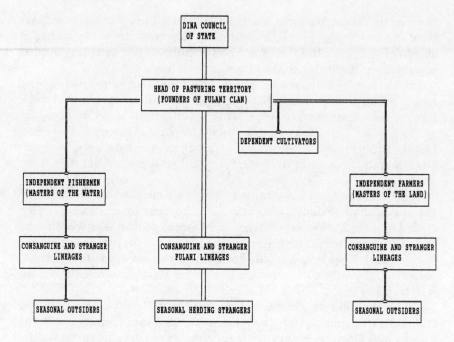

Figure 7.3   Political and administrative structures in the nineteenth century

herding, farming and fishing territories, to insist on the sedentarisa-
tion of the delta inhabitants (or at least oblige them to state the village
they came from), and to establish the order by which clan herds
entered their territory.

The *dina* system provided a management regime that coordinated
access to all resources in the delta. Three aspects of this regime were
important: first, it allowed for the movement of producers between and
within ecosystems at different moments of the year. Transhumant
herders followed established routes out to the drylands during the
rainy season and back through the millet-producing areas on their
return to the floodplains; farmer fishermen, agro-pastoralists and
farmers had reciprocal access rights to participate in the millet harvest
on the drylands, and the rice harvests on the floodplains; transhumant
fishermen and herders had established itineraries in moving through
the delta as the floodwaters retreated each year (CIPEA, 1983).

Second, the people who depended upon the resources of the delta to
subsist were also the managers: while in specific cases resources were
allocated within production systems (to marabouts) and between production systems (to *Rimaïbé* slave cultivators), the day-to-day management of access was carried out by the producers themselves. Third, it

coopted the fundamental principles of older delta land tenure systems: the primacy of the first-cover and the hierarchy of those who followed later. In areas where resources were re-allocated to new groups, the pre-eminence of the founding communities from whom the resources were taken was often reflected in their retention of the office of 'sacrificer'; within Fulani clans, the same system of founder, consanguine lineage and permanent/temporary stranger operated.

The resolution of conflict within this regime was carried out at three levels: at the level of the resource manager within production systems (clan head of the pasturing territory, master of the water, master of the land), at the level of pasturing territory or cantonnement between production systems, and at the level of the *dina* state for conflicts between territories and between cantonnements.

4. The evolution of property rights under colonial and independent administrations: sources of conflict

The colonial administration sought in the main to retain 'traditional' management regimes in the delta, but with two important differences. First, the Fulani hegemony in the area was broken early in the twentieth century, after long negotiations with Fulani leaders, the *Rimaïbé* status as 'slaves' was brought to an end. An administrative system of 'cantonnements' and 'cercles' was introduced, with each cantonnement being broadly based on the pasturing territory limits of the *dina* period.

Second, the French intervened directly in the management of access to the resources of the delta. Following the 'kitangal' drought of 1911–14 they instituted a management system for controlling the timing of transhumant herds through the delta, and also created a set of officially recognised fishing 'reserves'. Both these interventions were aimed at preserving resources until the end of the hot and dry season in the area of the lakes in the downstream areas of the delta.

While on the surface a traditional system seemed to be maintained, profound changes were taking place underneath. Of fundamental significance was:

(i)   That the ultimate authority in the area—the French administration—was not reliant itself on the resources of the delta to subsist.
(ii) It was uninformed about the area.
(iii) It was widely diffused—three French Commandants de Cercle administered the whole area from Djenné to Niafunké.

This meant that the basis for the authority of traditional cantonnement heads had significantly changed. Whereas before, their influence rested on membership in, or close linkages to, a dominant production system based on ethnic affiliation and religion (pastoralism, Fulani and Islam), under the French their power rested on the somewhat remote support of the colonial administration and their local ties. The colonial administration of the delta was Eurocentric in its ideology: freedom of slaves, equal access for the needy irrespective of status, ethnic affiliation, etc., and thus took little account of the existing indigenous organisation of society.

The effect on land tenure systems in the delta was to open former communally managed property to new users (for the most part coming from the same production system) who derived access not from the traditional authorities but by reference to the colonial administration (examples of this are given below). The customary authority of local- (village), as well as cantonnement-level resource managers began to be undermined. Colonial records speak frequently of the non-payment of tithes or rents as being cause for conflicts, these being for the most part between traditional managers of resources, seasonal visitors, or people who had settled in communities only recently (a 'stranger' remains an outsider in the delta even if his family has lived there for over a generation) (Gerbeau, 1957–8).

Since independence (1960) this process of 'opening' access to resources in the delta has accelerated and deepened, as parallel management structures have proliferated in line with the widening influence of the administration. Under the first post-independence government, that of Modibo Keita (1960–8), the customary heads of the cantonnements were replaced by centrally appointed 'chefs d'arrondissements', who were themselves strangers to the zone, and whose period of office in the area was short: this was accompanied by the launching of a cooperative movement that aimed to collectivise production and effectively placed economic power in the hands of urban-based officials of the movement. The forestry service, set up in the 1930s originally to safeguard wood fuel supplies to Niger river steamboats, saw its influence increase during this period to cover fisheries. Accompanying this process was a sustained ideological campaign against 'feudal' traditional authorities.

In 1972, under the second post-independence government of Moussa Traoré (1968 to 1991), the natural resources of Mali were nationalised, the powers of the forestry service were greatly increased with the publication of the forestry code, and several semi-autonomous 'Opérations de Développement' were created, these last being largely foreign-funded development projects intervening, in the case of the delta, in the domains of the fisheries, the livestock sector and agriculture. In the early 1980s, the sole political party in Mali was formed—the Union Democratique du Peuple Malien—with a structure of representation down to village level. In 1985–7 a structure for the management of 'development' was set up, drawing together the political party, village representatives, representatives of the technical services and the administration, in an effort to elicit grassroots support and policy initiatives, at the same time as a major government environmental policy was published, described as the national fight against desertification (PNLCD, 1987).

With this document, the government for the first time made a commitment to popular support for its development objectives. As part of this policy the government has launched a project to zone the whole extent of Mali according to 'agro-ecological' criteria with a view to defining environmentally sound development priorities for each region.

At the present time, therefore, there are three major structures with varying degrees of control over access to resources: the political party, the administration, and customary authorities. Further, within the administrative and political structure there are divisions at the local, regional and national level, and between different services (foresters, gendarmerie, Opérations de Développement, etc.). Figure 7.4 shows these relationships.

5. Present-day conflict in the delta

The desertification policy initiative comes at a time when customary methods for controlling access, and more modern parallel structures supposedly managing the land tenure systems in the inland Niger delta, are both in disarray. In the drought of 1973–4, and even more so during that of the early 1980s, the delta became an area of refuge both for its own inhabitants and for producers from neighbouring regions: as the resource base shrank, conflict which had for long been common at intermittent intervals, became endemic.

The context of present-day conflict over access to resources is specific. It is seasonal, inasmuch as it is concentrated in the period when the floodplains and drylands are respectively accessible, i.e. December–June in the wetlands and July–November in the drylands. It generally involves the same group of people—seasonal visitors to the zone, or 'strangers' who have resided for some time in a community, and local inhabitants. It takes place between members of the same

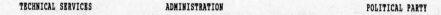

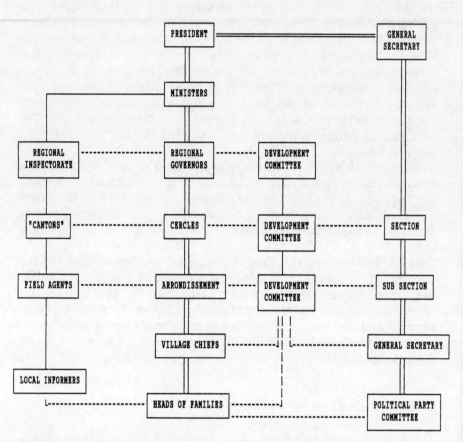

Figure 7.4   Political and administrative structures today

Note
Solid lines in this diagram refer to hierarchical links, dotted lines to consultative duties.

production system rather than across production systems, and it is most commonly found on the administrative boundaries of 'cercles'. By extension, it most often involves people from different administrative areas.

While the immediate cause of conflict is in many cases an urgent need for access because of the dry conditions, the possibility of an open clash (in which physical injury and fatalities often occur), and the ways in which such situations are exploited, owe much to the perennial *insecurity* of tenure delta inhabitants have over the resources they depend upon. This in turn is closely linked on the one hand to government policy in arbitrating land tenure disputes, and their philosophy in administering the zone, and on the other to a serious lack of coordination between elements of the state structure which, it might be argued, have some interest in promoting division within the area.

The Malian government attributes a right to rural inhabitants to exploit the usufruct of an area if they are the habitual inhabitants of a zone. But in administration they make no formal distinction between producers: for instance, any Malian citizen has a right to be a fisherman, and has a right of access to fisheries if he possesses a fishing permit, available to anyone from the forestry service on the payment of a sum of money. The administration, for the purposes of taxation, censuses and so forth, considers the population to be grouped in villages, or to be members of nomadic 'fractions', divided under a number of 'chefs de famille', who are the fiscal unit. In this manner, the basic assumptions of customary land tenure are denied: access to resources on the basis of ethnic and kinship allegiance and history of cohabitation within a community are not, formally, taken into account.

Further, there is no local administrative or political body with the effective power and responsibility to manage access to resources. The administrative 'cercle' is more often in competition with the local political party than in collaboration with it. Within the administrative hierarchy the respective technical services (foresters, gendarmerie, cooperative movement, livestock service) are equally in competition — often for access to informal payments made by local producers, which they are much in need of to make up for late payment of low salaries.

In general, local administrative policy, at a time when rural producers are finding it increasingly hard to make ends meet, is characterised by a concerted effort to raise taxes (with only limited success: in parts of the delta under 25% of the fiscal target was collected in 1984/5, although more was extracted unofficially by agents of the administration) (IUCN, 1989b).

While the technical services — in particular the forestry service — have a wide-ranging remit to protect the environment and monitor its use (as well as formidable powers to fine and imprison), they have neither the means nor the knowledge to function effectively. The areas they are asked to cover are vast, they have little transport, and their term of stay in any one zone (as with other administration officials) is short — rarely more than two years, so their perceived task is more one of game warden/tax man than conservationist.

It is not hard to see why conflict arises where local management customs and practices are not recognised, where the priority of local administrators and technical services is to raise revenue, and where several government structures are in competition, and where the doors are thrown open to a range of interests who want access to the resources of the area for short-term objectives. Conflict in the delta is often characterised by clashes between local producers who rely on their nearby resources, and those who visit the area each year to survive the dry season, but who come from other zones. In these conflicts local people find themselves confronted by economic interests often superior to their own, and whose strategies of production are to 'mine' the resources they get access to rather than consider their long-term viability. The following case study illustrates how the lack of a clear system of allocation of resources to people who can manage them fosters conflict in the inland delta.

6. Conflict in the fisheries of Lake Debo[2]

Some of the richest fisheries in the delta are found in the north-eastern part of the zone, in the region of Debo and Walado lakes. They are particularly productive when the water has drained off the floodplains, concentrating the fish in the main water courses and deep pools. During the dry season this area attracts between 7,000 and 10,000 outsider fishermen, who come to take part in the collective fisheries of the region. This is a brief account of what has happened to one set of these fisheries.

During the *dina* period, the area referred to here was owned by two masters of the water, living some five miles apart. In addition to reciprocal access rights to each of their fisheries, each territory had its traditional strangers whom it welcomed each year, and who came to fish in the river and later in the lakes each dry season: they generally visited their territories for two to three months annually.

Over the years a number of customary strangers had been assimilated into a downstream fishing camp beside the lake, and others had settled in more permanent camps along the main river. Some were from a different ethnic fishing group from the local people, but had the permission of local owners either to be part of the community or to settle where they had. In the early 1950s, a member of this stranger community, living in the camp beside the lake, was able to break the camp away from the traditional master of the water, by application to the head of the local cantonnement, and eventually through the French courts. This has meant that in recent years there have been three parties to conflict: locals, strangers and the administration, and the key to success has been access to the administration.

A period of comparative calm ensued for the next 20 years (a period of relatively good rainfall and flood levels). Then in the early 1970s, as conditions became more difficult, conflict broke out between the fishermen of the lakeside camp and the descendants of the pre-1952 master of the water. The administration was called in, and further diminished the authority of the original owners by allowing the use of senne nets in the area of water that remained under their control. The authorisation to use senne nets—exclusively used by outside fishermen—in effect gave greater rights of access to the strangers who had settled in fishing camps along the length of the river since the 1930s. In early 1981 further conflict broke out, as before between the downstream fishing camp and the former masters of the water, but this time including all the strangers in the other camps and the other masters of the water in the neighbouring fishing territory. The administration's answer to this was to open the entire length of river to any fishermen providing they agreed to local customs. Later in 1981 strangers and locals again came to blows and this time the governor of the region himself intervened. His decision was to keep the whole length of the fishery open to any fishermen, and further, to allow the use of sennes over the whole stretch of river: local customs, which were against the use of this technology, were further marginalised.

In the dry seasons of 1982, 1983 and 1984 there were violent incidents between local fishermen and strangers, leading at one moment to the police halting all fishing with senne nets for fear of the effect on public order. Late in 1984 the governor of the region annulled all previous edicts and stated categorically that the strangers on the river were allowed to use sennes. In 1986 conflict again broke out and strangers were only able to fish in the presence either of the police or foresters.

In 1987, faced with strong indications that the delta was being overfished, the administration instituted a new, region-wide fisheries policy, which banned the use of senne nets in many areas of the delta for part of the fishing season. The strangers avowed they would abide by local conditions for the time being, but that they would fight the decision at the level of central government.

Throughout this process, government records show local fishermen pleading their case with the local 'chef d'arrondissement' and 'commandant de cercle', while stranger fishermen, in some cases using family links, contacted the regional governor and ministries in the capital. What is significant is that the hierarchy of authority is respected by no one: the higher the person to whom they can appeal, the more likely they are to win their case.

What is not recorded, but is common knowledge on the ground, are the obligatory payments to all those in authority every time they are involved, by all conflicting parties. In this, local fishermen are at a disadvantage. Stranger fishermen from upstream come to the area with much more productive (and destructive) technology (senne nets of very small mesh size that reach right across the river) (ORSTOM, 1988) which (a) provide them with a much higher cash income, and (b) mean they are heavily in debt with net merchants in the towns. The net merchant/senne fisherman interest group is considerably more powerful in political and economic terms than locals, whose only recourse is simply to try and prevent them fishing.

7   Conclusion

In the inland Niger delta conflicts caused by changes in the environment are greatly exacerbated by the colonial legacy of administration of the people most closely reliant upon its production, and the needs of the post-colonial state itself. In the delta the policy of ignoring indigenous management systems—even a concerted effort to undermine them —has put the power to manage access to resources in the hands of those whose pressing short-term needs outweigh a long-term concern with the environment. On the one side are outside producers who only exploit the zone seasonally, and who can move on when the resources in one area are exhausted; and on the other are the civil servants whose stay in the area is short, and who need revenue to make up shortfalls in their salaries paid by the central government. Environmental conflict in the delta—in particular in the areas discussed here—thus confronts local inhabitants who will rely in the *long term* on the natural productivity of the zone, with those who use the area ephemerally, but who have powerful political links and pressing short-term economic aims.

At a higher level the requirements of the post-colonial state in Mali during these recent years of drought consist essentially in a need for revenue, either in the form of international aid or in terms of the formal and informal contributions of the country's citizenry. In terms of the productive base of the rural economy, for the last 15 years the inland delta has been an area of net disinvestment, in spite of the presence of major rural development projects in the region (IUCN, 1989b). Taxes and informal payments have raised rural producers' cash needs over and above the monetary requirements they have in bad years to buy essential foodstuffs on the market. This has contributed to abuse of the environment in order to make ends meet, while at the same time creating a serious credibility gap between rural producers and representatives of the administration. The raising of rural producers' cash needs generally feeds into both 'outsiders' and 'local' methods of exploiting the environment, and is an example of economic and fiscal policy provoking damaging use of the environment itself. This, in turn, further shrinks the resource base, creating the conditions for further conflict.

Local communities in the delta—particularly those found in the downstream, wetter areas—see government policy as aimed at depriving them of their traditional right to use and manage the areas they come from. Lacking in influence at the local, regional or central level their recourse is often to conflict with outside producers who, in turn, try (often successfully) to use their links with the administration to force access.

The situation described in this paper clearly shows the state unable to fulfil its traditional, Napoleonic function of standing above the sectarian interests of its component parts and acting in the name of the nation as a whole. As far as local producers are concerned, it might be likened to a vast 'founding' lineage wherein personal contact, through kinship ties and patron–client relationships, are manifestly more effective than following the formal hierarchies of the state structure. For them, the sole interest of the administration and its component parts is in the exaction of revenue, and they thus perceive the environmental policy, as it is presently exercised (primarily by the forestry service) as a means of taxation rather than as being related to the conservation of the environment.

It is hard to imagine how conflict over access to resources in the inland Niger delta can be resolved peacefully until a clear definition is made as to who owns what, and how, and it is difficult to see how such a definition can avoid incorporating those who know most about, and rely upon the local environment, if it is to arbitrate effectively between different producers' interests. Equally, it would be unrealistic to suppose that latter-day managers—the foresters, administration, political party—can or should be excluded from such a management system. During recent years of drought it has become increasingly clear that unless some attempt is made to reinvest some of what is taken out of the natural environment, long-term impoverishment will ensue (IUCN, 1989b). Unless at the local level new management structures come into being which represent the interests of those who rely upon the environment to survive, backed by consistent state support for their actions, the prospects for environmental conflict in areas of 'refuge' in Mali are serious.

The need for rural producers to gain access to resources both within their own ecosystems and in neighbouring areas is fundamental to their ability to adapt to the highly variable climatic conditions found in the Sahel. But where this movement entails conflict with host communities, undermines the hosts' own ability to gain their liveli-hoods, and threatens the sustainability of the resource upon which they depend, government policy should intervene to establish priori-ties over land use. This chapter has shown that the inability of the Malian state to stand above sectarian interests has been accompanied by an undermining of indigenous local land tenure systems, and has thrown open the door to 'mining' some of the delta's most productive assets by groups driven by indebtedness to urban merchants.

Given the unlikelihood of Mali developing a manufacturing or industrial sector to provide opportunities for rural inhabitants, future planning must be based on strengthening the subsistence sector: this in turn implies that attention should be focused on how the environ-ment can be managed sustainably in those areas of origin that are at risk of drought.

For this to come about, it would seem essential that the trend of disinvestment in production in the rural sector is reversed. It is un-likely that local support will be forthcoming for this unless rural producers are given clear title to their resources, and it is therefore suggested here that it is a precondition for the sustainable develop-ment of the delta that rural people be given secure land rights under-written by the *practice* of a consistent national development policy.

Notes

1. This work is based upon two periods spent in Mali: 1979–81, when the author was conducting research into the production system of the delta fishermen for an MA degree; 1984–8 when he was working on the IUCN project based in Youvarou, in the northern sector of the delta; and on further research carried out in Europe in 1989. The author would like to thank IUCN and their field staff in Mali for the opportunity to carry out this work, but would stress that the opinions this paper contains are his own.
2. This section relies on two sources: interviews with fishermen living in the area in question, both in 1980 and later; and research in the adminis-tration's archives in Mopti, the regional capital.

References

Miscellaneous government archives of the Mopti region, Mali.

CIPEA, 1983. *Recherche d'une solution aux problèmes de l'élévage dans le delta intérieur du Niger au Mali.* Rapport de Synthèse, vol. 5. CIPEA: Bamako.

ENDA, 1985. *La vie pastorale au Sahel. Initiation aux sociétés pastorales sahéliennes.* Report no. 1. ENDA: Dakar.

Gallais, J., (ed.) 1958. *La Vie saisonnière au sud du Lac Debo.* Mission d'étude et d'aménagement du Niger, Enquêtes géographiques no. 2. Service de l'Hydraulique de l'Afrique Occidentale Française, Dakar.

Gallais, J., 1967. *Le delta intérieur du Niger.* Étude de géographie régionale, 2 vols. IFAN: Dakar.

Gallais, J., 1984. *Hommes du Sahel.* Collections géographes. Flammarion: Paris.

Gerbeau, H., 1957–8. *La Région de l'Issa Ber.* Mission d'Étude et d'aménagement du Niger. Études de géographie humaine. Travaux Publics de la République Soudanaise: Dire, Mali.

IUCN, 1989a. *Rapport Final. Conservation de l'Environnement dans le Delta Interieur du Fleuve Niger.* IUCN: Gland, Switzerland.

IUCN, 1989b. *Rapport sur l'économie de la région de Mopti (Mali).* IUCN: Gland, Switzerland.

ORSTOM, 1988. *Enquête Statistique aupres des Pêcheurs: Études Halieutiques du delta central du Niger.* ORSTOM/INRZFH: Bamako.

PNLCD, 1987. *Le Plan Nationale de Lutte contre la Désertification et l'Avancée du Désert.* Ministère des Ressources Naturelles et de l'Elevage: Bamako.

RIM/ODEM, 1987. *Refuge in the Sahel: Livestock Populations and Production Systems in the Mali Fifth Region.* Ministère des Ressources Naturelles et de l'Elevage. Resource Inventory Management Limited: Jersey, UK.

8 Environmental Conflicts in African Arid Lands: Cases from the Sudan and Nigeria

M.A. Mohamed Salih

1. Introduction

The control, use and management of any given environment often perpetuate contradictory interests in resource endowments which may result in environmental conflicts. Such conflicts are by no means new and cannot be seen as mere products of present-day processes of development or in isolation from the historical sequence within which they have occurred. What has happened in recent decades is an unprecedented intensification of environmental crises pertaining to population growth, an accelerating drive towards commercialism and an excessive expansion of modern production techniques.

Environmental concerns have, therefore, overshadowed the political arena in the West, the East and the South and have in addition contributed to an upsurge of ecology groups and national and international environmental agencies and organizations. Moreover, environmental awareness began to spread across the Third World countries, creating major conflicts between societal interests and economic gains. In the Third World, environmental conflicts have been engendered by the quest for accelerated economic change which has invited the implementation of short-term development plans. Such development efforts have, in some cases, inflicted serious environmental crises represented in differences in production objectives at local and national levels. Some development plans have alienated the majority of small producers through an inequitable allocation of the most valuable natural resources to the few wealthy and powerful. This in turn has prompted economic and social differentiation and divided the population into 'haves' and 'have nots'. Problems of poverty, exclusion from means of livelihood and the subsequent struggle to break out of the poverty circle and to secure access to resources are often expressed, either in peaceful political actions or in violent protests, unrest and rebellious movements. It is so close to people's hearts that the struggle for the environment is a struggle for survival and it is only because of this notion that the political dimension of resource allocation becomes pertinent in defining how the environment is conceptualized by different actors. Thence the claim that the association between environmental and political conflicts is a new phenomenon is erroneous and baseless. It is a relationship which has existed since the dawn of history, albeit in different forms and socio-political contexts.

Today, there are numerous publications and reports on the relationship between environmental conflicts and the political milieu within which such conflicts emerge. In the majority, social scientists have implicit or explicit references to a political economy of environmental crisis. This is so because any attempt to understand the causes of pollution, famine, the effect of droughts and desertification discerns an agenda inspired by a political economy. Such an agenda usually explicates the main class of beneficiaries and losers in the process. This, nevertheless, is not to claim that the political problems emanating from environmental conflicts are associated with specific forms of political structure: capitalism, socialism, private or collective ownership. Such a claim cannot be empirically defended or theoretically justified. Environmental concerns are not system-specific either in politics or economics and their prevalence has been felt in almost all political systems, capitalist and socialist, and in all countries developed as well as underdeveloped. Moreover, dwelling on establishing a relationship between environmental conflicts and politics is of no theoretical or practical value for its own sake, mainly because no viable solutions can be attained by the mere proof or disproof of the incidence of such an association. What is important in this respect is the manner in which environmental conflicts can be pernicious to security, if security is given a wider meaning than military security.

The following preliminary postulates could be derived from the above introduction and are hoped to enhance the discussion in this direction. First, environmental conflicts are products of certain dynamics which differ from one society to another. However, there is no evidence to suggest that such dynamics are present in all types of political organization. For example, in highly industrialized societies, the environmental crisis is a product of an 'economy versus society' syndrome. In this case, high productivity and economic efficiency, and high profitability rather than environmental concern, dominate over societal interests in a clean environment. Such production systems as those of the developed countries may in some instances sacrifice societal interests for those of dominant groups in the state. Hence, the human imperative is seen as secondary to profit and greed.

Nevertheless, economy seems to rule, when it comes to the environment, even in the socialist countries which are much more concerned with questions of equitable distribution of goods and services. The available evidence reveals that there are poorer environmental protection measures in some socialist countries than in the industrially advanced capitalist economies. The cutting of wood for charcoal-making, fencing and house-building and extending the grazing and cultivation of land are not matters of carelessness on the part of poor peasants and pastoralists in underdeveloped countries, but a matter of poor people in a continuous struggle to eke out a living in a situation of absolute poverty and destitution. The greed of the rich and their desire for profit regardless of environmental consequences is just as damaging to the environment as the poverty of the rural masses. In 'Third World' countries like those of Africa, and the drylands, in particular, environmental conflicts could likewise be engendered by the strife for survival determined by poverty and other production and social constraints hindering adherence to appropriate systems of resource utilization and maintenance.

Second, environmental conflicts are interrelated to the extent that it is impossible to divide the world into fragmented regions hoping that one nation or continent would survive the consequences of a major disaster. Hence the struggle for the environment and the political means available to pursue such a struggle are expressions of a common struggle for the survival of the human race. Hence, the present environmental predicament is a product of a political and economic organization which survives on the reproduction of the very depleting production objectives and techniques which are leading to dangerous consequences.

Third, environmental conflicts are far-reaching and usually outgrow so-called local and national boundaries and outstrip the capacity of any individual society to solve them independently. For instance, the impact of any nuclear fall-out would be felt all over Europe and beyond. Likewise, the impacts of famine and drought have already been felt not only in the Third World countries, but in the living rooms, TV screens, streets, and even in the bank accounts of many citizens in the economically prosperous parts of the world who have made generous donations to remedy the plight of the hungry and the destitute. In the seemingly simple, but humanistic sense, environmental conflicts have been capable of reviving a sense of humanity which is more needed today than ever before.

With these points in mind, the theme of this chapter is therefore that it is premature to associate environmental conflicts with climatic changes or ecological imbalances without reference to the political processes which mediate or have triggered them off in the first place. Hjort and Mohamed Salih (1989, p. 11) argue that

conventional politically and ideologically motivated models are not sufficient to redress the problems of the vulnerable sectors of the population and the victims of ecological degradation. Concepts such as entitlement and sustainability enter the picture, since issues of deprivation and impoverishment require viable solutions and they are closely interrelated.

Within this perspective, I intend to explore the political impacts of environmental conflicts and their effects on ecology, polity and society in African drylands, with special reference to the Sudan and Nigeria.

2. Africa's environmental crisis and the dryland

African arid lands extend from the edge of the tropics to the dry deserts. They embrace almost whole countries such as Niger, Mauritania, Mali and Chad and over 60–70% of the Sudan, Ethiopia, Kenya, Tanzania, Somalia, Botswana and Namibia. Including the Sahara desert and North Africa, the drylands claim between 80–100% of Egypt, Libya, Morocco and Algeria. None of the remaining African states is without a region which can be described as arid or semi-arid. The Soudano-Sahelian countries, in particular, have suffered successive and tragic drought phases during the last two decades. These drought periods are depicted by Rasmusson (1987), who points out that

rain fluctuations in Africa during recent years are as follows: a) wet conditions throughout Africa during the 1950s, b) a severe pattern of drought (a situation where rain is below what is normally needed or expected for crop and livestock production) during 1968–1973, with abnormally dry conditions prevailing throughout Africa except for a narrow equatorial strip (Nicholas, 1985), c) an easing of dry conditions during the remainder of the 1970s followed by a return to extreme drought conditions over much of the continent during 1982–1984.

The main subsistence activities in the drylands include arable cropping and pastoralism, for which a minimum of 400 mm of rain are needed depending on the availability of drought-resistant crop varieties. Other subsistence activities such as hunting and collecting and gathering are prevalent even though they have begun to lose their significance. The main crops cultivated in the drylands include sorghum, millet, groundnuts, cotton, sesame, hibiscus and a variety of other minor crops. Livestock such as cattle, goats and sheep are kept as a wealth reserve and status symbol or exchanged for cash. Crop failures or livestock loss during long drought spells upset the normal rhythm of life, induce migration to other alien regions or towns and centres of employment, and create uncertainty and fear for life. During drought one observes a decrease in other activities such as gathering of various wild edible plant species and hunting, while the cutting of trees for charcoal and firewood is often intensified.

The present crisis in the African drylands reveals that environmental conflicts can occur with or without technological change and even during normal climatic conditions. Furthermore, it points out that the so-called 'Third World' countries are following the same pattern of development and perceive their future to be a replica of what is taking place in the industrial world today. The inevitability of such discourse is manifold and cannot easily be dismissed by romanticizing the simplicity of techniques and modes of livelihood amongst small-scale societies in the arid lands.

First, although they are poor in terms of natural endowments, the drylands have long been incorporated into the logic and rationality of the market economy. Governmental controls, which have begun since the colonial legacy, were accompanied by the creation of marketing boards trading in the export of gum-arabic, groundnuts, livestock products, cotton and oil seeds. These processes have been reinforced during independence through structural political and economic dependence between the African states and their ex-colonizers. An important point to make is that such economic institutions had in some cases not given way to industrialization or major change in the techniques of production.

Second, African agrarian policies are more concerned with the modern commercial export-oriented sector, with less emphasis on food crops. With little or no improvements in the traditional sector, peasant communities have been forced to split their labour between cash and food-earning activities. The former included activities such as the production of cash crops and migration to towns and centres of employment which have stripped the rural areas of the best of their productive forces. The allocation of financial resources and investment has in all African countries favoured cash crops and the modern agricultural sector.

Third, in some countries the expansion of private and state-owned large-scale mechanized agricultural schemes, plantations and mining activities has meant that vast stretches of land have been appropriated from traditional producers and allocated to the modern sector. As a result, environmental conflicts are intensified not only between the modern and the traditional sectors, but also between peasants and pastoralists within the traditional systems of land use.

Fourth, externally, the situation is aggravated by the drop in the prices of primary commodities and a relatively high increase in the prices of imported manufactured goods. This has contributed to the alienation of rural households from their production and hence relegated many of them to poverty and destitution. In retrospect this means that more land has had to be put under production, not to improve standards of living, but to maintain the *status quo*. Some cases in this chapter illustrate that a depleted countryside cannot readily afford the labour nor the land required for such an undertaking.

These policies, coupled with the environmental crisis, have resulted in huge food shortages in Africa. The statistics of agricultural production in Africa reveal that self-sufficiency in cereals decreased from 83% in 1973 to 73% in 1982 and is destined to fall further to about 56% in the year 2000. In 1986/7, Africa spent 5.4 billion dollars on financing its cereal deficit alone. With the present African economic crisis, it is estimated that Africa will soon assign more than 30% of its exports to food importation. These facts may relate more to the political economy of food production than to environmental crisis, which may equally well be aggravated by the fact that little or no food surplus could be extracted from a stagnating agrarian sector whose main objective is to produce cash crops for export.

The above are only hints pointing to the unprecented distortions and pressures within which the traditional systems of production operate. The outcome of these processes is that peasant and pastoral communities became more and more dependent on and susceptible to fluctuations in the market economy. Furthermore, they are under continuous pressures from governmental policies and ill-planned agricultural development projects. It is obvious that the peasants and pastoralists have become even more vulnerable to ecological imbalances and less capable of producing surplus food to safeguard themselves against low harvests.

3. Technological change and environmental conflicts in the Sudan

Technological change is not only a technical solution to the constraints of production, it is a carrier of social and political biases in terms of who owns it and what sector of the population is more vulnerable to its consequences. Furthermore, technology mediates the political arrangements of the society and in its quest for efficiency it often produces undesirable impacts regardless of the scale of operation and the natural resource endowment to be harnessed. The Sudan case is a clear example of the way agrarian change through the importation of inappropriate technology can produce far-reaching environmental and political conflicts, and re-defines the existing system of social stratification by creating masses of rural poor versus the wealthy holders of large-scale mechanized agricultural schemes.

The Sudan is the largest country in Africa. It covers 2.5 million square kilometres and supports a population of about 22 millions according to the 1983 population census. Agriculture and livestock raising are the main sources of livelihood for about 80–5% of the population; 35% of the GDP is derived from agriculture, while agricultural exports represent about 75% of the country's foreign exchange earnings. The agricultural sector can be divided into four main subsectors. Large-scale mechanized irrigated state-owned schemes, large-scale mechanized rain-fed private schemes, traditional irrigation and traditional rain-fed farming systems. The state-owned large-scale mechanized irrigated and the private rain-fed schemes are market-oriented while the traditional sub-sector is geared towards subsistence where very little surplus could be produced or marketed. By 1986/7 the modern sector, both irrigated and rain-fed, comprised over 40% of the total area under cultivation, i.e. about 4 million hectares.

In this section I shall deal mainly with the impact of the introduction of large-scale mechanized agricultural schemes in the drylands of the Sudan and their environmental impacts. The development of private large-scale agricultural schemes dates back to the colonial legacy when the Anglo-Egyptian condominium rule (1898–1956) introduced large-scale government-managed schemes in Gedarif, Eastern Sudan. Adam et al. (1983) note that between 1945 and 1953 allotments to share-croppers did not survive because of permanent settlement difficulties manifested by the seasonality of production and the inadequacy of the requisite infrastructure. The second phase continued from 1953 to 1968 and, due to a shortage of public capital finance, the private sector was involved through a leasehold system. This system was described as being open to abuse and dominated by rich farmers, notables and senior government officers.

When the Mechanized Farming Corporation was established in 1968, its mandate was to survey and prepare land for large-scale mechanized farming and to facilitate credit services for financially able farmers. Farmers were given leaseholds for 25 years for 1,500 feddans (1 hectare equals 2.38 feddans). Large stretches of land were appropriated from traditional cultivators and pastoralists. The clearance of trees for the new schemes has devastated gum arabic revenues, an important source of income for the local population and the country, and game (such as giraffe, antelopes, guinea fowl, hyenas, zebra, etc.) disappeared either by extermination or migration to the south.

The third phase in the expansion of the large-scale mechanized schemes continues from 1968 until today with two major differences. First, the emergence of illegal acquisition of land by wealthy merchants in remote areas and without the knowledge of the government. The Sudan policy of encouraging the importation of agricultural machinery such as tractors and combine disc harvesters has meant that tractors were excepted from import taxes. Second, the plan whereby the Sudan should become the bread-basket of Africa and the Middle East encouraged the rich Arab oil-producing countries to extend soft loans to the Sudan.

The unplanned expansion of large-scale mechanized schemes created havoc among small producers, both peasants and pastoralists. With an annual demand for 100,000 casual labourers, many traditional producers were transformed into wage labourers working for the very people who appropriated their lands. Those whose villages have been completely surrounded by the schemes have been transformed into landless rural poor. The same awkward situation applies to pastoralists who lost their animal routes, water points and grazing lands to private owners. It is estimated that 40% of the population living adjacent to the large-scale mechanized schemes began to experience shortages of fertile cultivable lands from 1980 onwards, while 80% of the 350,000 pastoralists in the Southern Kordofan Province are negatively affected. A similar prospect was observed by Wani (1987, pp. 102–3), who argues that

One reason why these schemes were close to the villages was that the scheme owners were often illegally expanding farm land into areas considered as village lands. Sometimes it was the local Dinka elites who come from these villages who would cultivate this land, arguing that if they did not cultivate this land, merchants would appropriate it. In practice, the local population has been squeezed on both sides by the scheme owners and the village elites, who usually have their bases in the urban centres.

The situation in the South is no different from that described by Ahmed (1987, p. 137) in the savannah belt in the southern parts of the White Nile and the Blue Nile provinces in central Sudan. Ahmed (ibid.) points out that

conflicts between pastoral nomads and sedentary cultivators are becoming the major problem facing the administration of the region. These conflicts have been more complicated and their frequency has increased through the challenge introduced by the agricultural development plans.

I argue elsewhere (Mohamed Salih, 1987, p. 3) that

planned agrarian change in the rainlands has not taken into account the complexity of the eco-system, the traditional agricultural and pastoral production systems and the likely impact that it might have on society, economy and ecology.

This argument still stands valid for that which I develop in the present work with more emphasis on environmental conflicts.

In environmental terms, the stated policy of creating large-scale mechanized schemes without due consideration to the traditional systems of livelihood, has led to population and livestock concentration in smaller areas than before. The end result is grievous. Over-grazing and over-cultivation have occurred, with negative impacts on the carrying capacity of pasture and cultivable lands. This in turn means that some of the traditional practices which used to alleviate pressure on land, such as shifting cultivation and co-ordinated long-distance transhumant life are no longer possible. In economic terms, it means less livestock and farm productivity and a lowering of the living standards of local producers. In technological terms, it is obvious that the economies of scale, other things being equal, are detrimental to the small producers, who cannot compete with the large-scale producers. In some instances, small producers are forced to sell their crops immediately at very low prices during the harvesting season in order to meet pressing household needs. The prices of the same crops would double a few months after the harvesting season, with the loss of large profits to the wealthy merchants/farmers.

The large-scale mechanized schemes have created their own environmental problems. The commercial farming practised by private farmers does not give any priority to resource maintenance or preservation. The rotation system which has been devised by the Mechanized Farming Corporation has not been practised and the wind barriers which were to be planted to prevent soil erosion and to maintain the stability of underground water were not implemented by the scheme owners, whose prime interest is to extract high profits from the land. The loss of fertile soils and the decline of the water level and land productivity were documented (Galal el-Din, 1974; O'Brien, 1978; Ibrahim, 1978, 1984; Kadouf and Mohamed Salih, 1986). However, the private owners' answer to the decline in land productivity is to open up new areas, clear more forests and continue with the same agricultural practices: this means that more land has been ruined and more forests cleared. As land productivity decreases and the profit margin is squeezed, the price of hired labour and the incomes of the agricultural labourers decrease sharply. Many of the local population who were self-sufficient a few years ago, have been reduced to ruin or rural poverty. It is a vicious circle demonstrating the association between environmental conflicts on one hand and their impact on the economic pursuits of the population on the other. The political dimension of this process is certainly linked with the way deprivation of the use of landed resources may lead to political conflicts.

The most glaring example of the transformation of environmental conflicts into political conflicts is the emergence of three regional political movements within the area where the large-scale mechanized schemes are allocated: the Sudan Peoples Liberation Army and Sudan Peoples Liberation Movement (SPLA/SPLM), the General Union of the Nuba Mountain (GUNM) and the Ingessena General Union (IGU). The SPLA/SPLM is a Southern-based national political movement which aims among other things to rid the Sudanese of the exploitative nature of the present political system, which is characterized by a Northern hegemony over the rest of the Sudanese nationalities. With its declared political bias towards the underdeveloped regions of the country, the SPLA/SPLM has enjoyed the political support of many Nuba and Ingessana peoples. The Nuba and the Ingessena began as early as 1985 attacking some of the private large-scale mechanized schemes in the Nuba Mountains, Southern Kordofan and the southern parts of the Blue Nile Province. These attacks were co-ordinated with SPLA/SPLM forces, halting production in the large-scale mechanized schemes in the northern parts of Bahr el-Ghazal province. The large-scale mechanized schemes were targeted because of what is expressed in the objectives of the General Union of the Nuba Mountains as to 'eradicate the feudalistic land policies and relations of production'. The reference here is to the fact that most of the owners of the large-scale mechanized schemes belong to the wealthy merchants and political elites from the northern parts of the Sudan known locally as *Jellaba*. It is also an expression of the association between the faulty distributive mechanisms deployed by the state and the real needs of the population who were not reached by 'development'.

The Sudan case reveals three sets of interrelated processes emanating from the impact of technology on agrarian change. First, as certain segments of the population have access to modern farm technology, which requires vast cultivable lands, the poorer segments can easily be deprived of their sources of livelihood. Land gained by the rich is land lost by the poor. Second, environmental conflicts can be worsened both physically and socially by the introduction of an inappropriate technology. Physically, land degradation is no longer confined to the traditional producers with their limited land use practices, it is aggravated by the use of an advanced technology more capable of devastating larger areas and at a more accelerated rate. Third, as the struggle for the control and use of a given environment intensifies, the real engagement of the populace is swayed from livelihood concerns to vigorous political movements capable of shattering political stability and challenging security. In the Sudanese case thousands of lives have been lost because of war and famine in the Nuba Mountains and the southern parts of the Blue Nile since the civil war began in 1983. I believe that if the SPLA/SPLM is fighting for genuine political grievances, the Nuba and the Ingessena are fighting for grievances emanating directly from the manner in which the environment has been controlled and administered by the central government.

It is premature to claim that environmental conflicts in the Sudan have occurred only as a result of technological change. The 1972/5 and 1983/5 drought spells gave rise to serious conflicts over landed resources in the rich southern savannah. Out-migration from drought-stricken areas to less affected areas have contributed to inter-ethnic conflicts over the available land resources. The Sudanese state entered the picture as a protector of the agricultural policies which it has implemented in the central arid lands. Mass migration to the southern parts of the central rainlands means that some type of land reform has to be carried out by the government to accommodate the newcomers. The state was not only in confrontation with the interest of the victims of drought, it has eventually prevented them from being independent of its whim.

By then, many drought and famine victims were forced to move to the urban centres looking for employment or to be close to relief agencies. Town planning committees, on the other hand, resisted their so-called illegal residence and the mushrooming of shanty towns and squatter settlements. A massive wave of what is termed internal or environmental refugees can today be felt in all large urban centres in the Sudan. As the struggle for access to more fertile lands continued in rural areas, the urban refugees intensified their struggle as they have to confront severe shortages of services and food in the urban centres.

I argue elsewhere (Mohamed Salih, 1989, pp. 113–14) that the Sudanese experience has shown that a state under external (financial constraints, debt burden, unequal exchange, etc.) and internal (underdevelopment, economic crisis, drought, famine, etc.) pressures is incapable of properly and completely solving the problems emanating from ecological stress. Hence, the state's effort to deal with development has been diverted to one of survival management. Since survival requires certain structural and infrastructural amenities, in which most African states are lacking, the general tendency has so far been the deployment of coercive measures to curtail the undesirable consequences of ecological stress. This is true in as much as the Sudanese state has continuously used the army and the police to halt any spontaneous settlement in areas which it has demarcated for the wealthy and powerful farmers. Further coercive measures have included the destruction of the mud and cardboard houses of the urban refugees and their repatriation by force to the so-called *Kasha* institution.

The two Sudanese examples reveal that environmental conflicts can have different facets and they may occur as a result of both natural disasters and technological change. In the two cases one can easily discern a linkage between technological change and the way it has created at least two types of conflict. The first set of conflicts is within the areas surrounding the large-scale mechanized schemes, while the second is the far-reaching impacts of technological change on distant small producers and in halting their movement to more fertile lands during times of great stress and need.

4. Environmental conflicts in Northern Nigeria

In contrast to the Sudan, Nigeria is considered one of the richest oil-producing countries in Africa. With a population of about 98 million, Nigeria's GDP comprises 26.1% agriculture, 17% petroleum, 17% trade and 11% manufacturing. However, petroleum is the main export commodity, totalling over 80% of total exports. Although annual food imports are rising, only 79.5 million acres of the 231 million acres of cultivable lands are utilized. The under-utilization of the cultivable lands is due to the structure of land ownership, availability and accessibility of farming technology and other problems related to the political and social organization of the agrarian structure. Nevertheless, like the Sudan, Nigeria has embarked on ostentatious agricultural development programmes. These include the river basin schemes, private rain-fed farms and rural development projects aimed at reaching middle-range farmers through the provision of agricultural inputs and credit. Despite an impressive investment in the agricultural sector, Nigeria suffered food shortages estimated at 553 thousand tons in 1982 and about 6.8 thousand tons in 1985. This is attributed mainly to the fact that the allocation of development funds was concentrated in the market-oriented sector, mainly cotton, tobacco and groundnuts. This policy created a negative impact and resulted in a huge food deficit. The same applies to livestock production, where Nigerians consume 20% less than the minimum proteins required. This is so although Nigeria has about 11 million head of cattle, over 20 million goats and more than 9 million sheep. In fact, Nigeria's meat and dairy imports account for 16% of the total domestic food supply.

Since agriculture and livestock production are the main sources of food supply, they both respond negatively to drought, especially in Northern Nigeria where the rainfall is less predictable. However, ecological imbalance in Northern Nigeria is not a new phenomenon. Official reports indicate that drought was recorded since 1914 and a rinderpest epidemic was recorded in 1948 (Watt, 1983, 1987). The recent drought spells of 1972/4 and 1983/4 are documented in Derrick (1977, 1984) and Apaldoorn (1981).

These two drought spells occurred in the northern states of Nigeria, mainly Sokoto, Kano, northern Kaduna, Katsina and Borno. This region is called the Sudanic zone and is inhabited mainly by Hausa farmers and Fulani pastoralists. The population of the five states is over 20 million, with a population density of about 80 people per square kilometre, which is among the most densely populated regions in Africa. The main activities, as in other parts of the Sahelian zone, include livestock raising and arable cultivation. According to Apeldoorn (1981, p. 27)

resource management in areas like the Nigerian Sudanic zone are functionally adapted to the environment. But at the same time these equalibria between people and their environment, although worked out in long periods of trial and error, are far from static; change in one or more factors makes the modification of any such system inevitable.

Such change was triggered off by long spells of drought which upset the traditional basis of resource management and created harsh new realities as living conditions degenerated from self-sufficiency in food to bare survival or starvation.

One of the serious impacts of drought in Northern Nigeria, according to Nnoli (1989, p. 171) is that

Nigeria not only has to battle with desertification and its victims in its northern states of Sokoto, Katsina, Kano and Borno, it has also to contend with similar victims from Niger, Chad and Mali.

Drought therefore has resulted in massive population mobility from the savannah to the sub-humid zone where the rains are more reliable. It appears that some of the river basin development schemes are contributory factors in the exodus of small peasants and pastoralists. The schemes were located in the northern states which have high human and livestock population density. As in the Sudan, vast stretches of land which were traditionally used by traditional pro- ducers for subsistence or pasture are now used for the production of cash crops for export. The particular case of the Fulani pastoralists, who own about 85% of livestock in Nigeria, is depicted by Udo (1979), who comments that 'the mechanized schemes were expanded at the expense of the Fulani pastures and it had thus created conflicts between the pastoralists and the cultivators.' Okaiyeto (1982, p. 529) argues that,

the river basin development authorities have concentrated until 1978/1979 only on crop production. This focus suggests that most of the Fulani traditional grazing lands have been transformed into arable lands. The end result of this ill-conceived policy is that the Fulani would then become marginal farmers at best, and at worst, landless labourers working for the governing bureaucratic and other elites.

This indicates that a process of differentiation has emerged with a clear demarcation of wealthy farmers with access to capital, finance and modern technology on one hand, and marginal farmers and pastoralists on the other. As in the case of the Sudan, conflicts began to emerge at two levels: first, the rich/poor divide as pointed out by Beckman (1985, p. 128) as many farmers lost their lands to the schemes. He argues that,

struggles culminated in the 1979–1980 dry season, when farmers stopped the contractors from operating for several months and obstructed current farm operations, including disconnecting sprinkler pipes. Road blocks were mounted and guarded by detachments of farmers armed mostly with cutlasses, bows and arrows, and other traditional weapons. Farmers demanded compensation for lost land and crops and asserted their right to decide what to grow, when to grow it, and how. In April 1981 the state let loose the paramilitary and the police force which brutally suppressed the rebellion, burning villages and killing and wounding hundreds of men, women and children.

The second set of conflicts emerged between peasants and pastoralists in the river basin schemes as no services were rendered to the pastoralists. Hassan (1987, p. 181) asserts that

no significant services were provided to the pastoral Fulbe by the river basin authority since its inception 11 years ago. Instead, the pastoral Fulbe are suffering increasing alienation from land and water shortages, increasing conflict with farmers, emergence of new cattle diseases and/or an increase in the existing cattle diseases.

There is a clear indication that the technological package proposed by the planners did not consider seriously the intricacy of the man/land/livestock ratio and the danger of concentrating vast stretches of land in a few hands. The situation is one of multiple conflicts: environmental, political and social, which involve the state and the wealthy farmers on the one hand, and the small producers, both peasants and pastoralists, on the other.

The position of the Fulani pastoralists of Northern Nigeria, who represent the largest pastoralist group in Western Africa, has an intimate relationship with the environmental issues of the drylands.

The Fulani live throughout the Sahelian zone and like other pastoralists they adopt a transhumant way of life and migrate from one ecological zone to another. Their movement is organized in accordance with the seasons and variations in rainfall and pasture. The Fulani pastoralists and the settled population interact in the market and in their competition for the *fadamas* (valleys and lowlands) which the pastoralists use as dry-season pasture. Since the pastoralists have no title to land, they are always in conflict with the farmers over the use of the *fadamas* and other landed resources. The pastoralists, therefore, are in fierce competition with the farmers and hence the use of the most productive land in the northern states.

One way out for the pastoralists was sought in the establishment of grazing reserves. This development activity began since the late 1940s under the auspices of the International Bank for Reconstruction and Development (IBRD) and was carried out by the FAO-supported programme in 1953. By 1985, only 22 million hectares of land had been acquired and demarcated as grazing reserves, all of it in the northern states. The main thrust came after the 1970s' drought phase with the main objective of securing pasture for the Fulani pastoralists, who would otherwise be subjected to an increasing pressure on land and subsequent drought and food shortages in the northern Sudanic drylands. The overall policy was designed against the following background:

(i)   Land tenure in Nigeria is such that the Fulani have no legal rights to the traditional grazing lands which they have been using for centuries. The Fulani are said to have migrated to Northern Nigeria or what is known in the literature as Hausaland. The grazing reserves are thus planned to protect the Fulani against the expanding agricultural sector and the posibility that they may end up as landless pastoralists, a process similar to the proletarianization of the peasants.

(ii)   The grazing reserves are envisaged as a sound solution to the environmental problems with which the Fulani are confronted by providing them with permanent water points, pasture, and services to control disease and epidemics. In short, the settlement of the Fulani pastoralists is expected to alleviate pressure on land and avail vast stretches of cultivable lands for the production of badly needed food crops.

None the less, the grazing reserves have created their own environmental conflicts, which take at least three forms:

(i)   The pastoralists were confronted by the farming communities, who perceived in the Fulani immigration a threat to their land and future farm expansion. Many Hausa farmers continued farming in their old farms within the grazing reserves. In this sense the land tenure issue has not been resolved and conflicts between traditional producers are still thriving.

(ii)　The Fulani pastoralists are again squeezed in smaller stretches of land. The process of monitoring and preventing their cattle from damaging the farms became almost a labour-intensive activity. This has also created a new set of problems, as the conflicts between Fulani pastoralists and Hausa farmers has intensified.

(iii)　Ecologically, the concentration of livestock in the grazing reserves and the very services that were provided have contributed to over-grazing. Over-cultivation has also occurred, as the population has tripled in a short span of time.

There is no doubt that the grazing reserves have not offered appropriate compensation for the traditional grazing lands which the pastoralists have already lost to the river basin schemes and other sub-sectors of the modern agrarian structure. In the face of this, they are threatened by several calamities resulting from increasing insecurity: first, the question of what the future holds for them when more lands are requisitioned for agricultural expansion as the population increases by 3% every year. Second, insecurity with respect to the lack of any livelihood alternatives *vis-à-vis* the present agricultural policies, which pay lip service to the pastoralists but do not take any concrete action.

Despite Nigeria's huge oil revenues during the early 1980s, independence and oil, according to Shenton (1986, p. 139) have together shattered the illusion of stability; and the development dream of the 1960s has, for many, become a nightmare. Hunger stalks the cities and countryside, the bounty from oil providing only a fragile shield in the form of food imports. It is obvious that the mishandling of the wealth generated by oil was one of the factors which contributed to the demise of small producers in Northern Nigeria. Moreover, the colonial state was successful only in draining the country's resources—resources which could otherwise have been used for the development of the country. Neo-colonialism is no different in pursuit and practice. Watt (1987, p. 194) observes that when drought hit the northern parts of Nigeria, some of the small producers were already drained by taxation and the exploitative market mechanism.

Again the case of Northern Nigeria reveals that environmental conflicts may occur as a consequence of the introduction of technological change whose effects are not confined to a particular region. When weighed against their benefits, the unintended negative environmental impacts are seen to be detrimental to security and development. The fact that Nigeria has been transformed from a food-producing country to a major food-importing country in Africa is explicit evidence for such a conception.

5. Conclusion

The cases of the Sudan and Nigeria demonstrate that environmental conflicts are pervasive in nature. They normally transcend climatic abnormality to affect the very basis of the survival of states and people alike. In a largely land-based economy like that of Africa, landed resources are the foci of economic and political activities. The alienation of one sector of the community from these resources is a potential source of conflict.

In a sense, environmental conflicts are multi-dimensional and work their way through various levels of the local, national, regional and international structure. Such a conception may suggest that there is an urgent need to go beyond the mere description of environmental conflicts to issues pertaining to minimizing if not eliminating them altogether. The creation of a dualistic economy: one for the reproduction of subsistence and the other for the national and international markets reflects a tendency towards internationalization of the environment which is no longer beyond the reach of the multi-nationals and centres of economic and political whim. Appealing to humanitarian gestures alone should not suffice in the efforts to develop a more equitable system of sharing with the whole, the surplus resources of some parts of the world. Even such innocent and seemingly naive ideas have to be supported by the very political powers which have contributed to the demise of the poor classes or nations.

It is ironic that environmental conflicts in the Third World have intensified through the use of the very technology which was introduced to promote food production. Inappropriate technological change has contributed to environmental degradation and has induced conflicts between the traditional and the modern sectors of the agrarian structure. Conflicts in which the state machinery is consciously deployed not to redeem the suffrage of the victims and the destitute, but to further the accumulation of land and its concentration in the hands of the few, wealthy and powerful. Again, both in their face value and essence, environmental conflicts are nothing but reflections of an inherent power struggle over the control of the environment in a largely land-based economy. Industrialization may equally well contribute to the transformation of environmental conflicts to class conflicts which require complex systems of control to contain undesirable effects and minimize their social cost. Both ways, the human imperative is sacrificed for different systems of dominance, one close to the natural environment and the other removed from its subsistence nature and subsumed under the wider world-system. The struggle for environmental security, therefore, has its price, and the question is, who is prepared to bail humanity out of the dangerous habit of ruining the environment and rid it of the subsequent economic, social and political calamities?

References

Adam, F.H. et al., 1983. 'Mechanized agriculture in the central rainlands of the Sudan', in P. Oesterdiekhoff and K. Wohlmuth (eds), *The Development Perspective of the Republic of the Sudan*. Weltform Verlag: Munich.

Ahmed, A.M., 1987. 'National ambivalence and national hegemony: the neglect of the nomads in the Sudan', in M.A. Mohamed Salih (ed.) *Agrarian Change in the Central Rainlands, Sudan*. Scandinavian Institute of African Studies: Uppsala.

Apaldoorn, G.J. Van, 1981. *Perspectives on Drought and Famine in Nigeria*. George Allen and Unwin: London.

Awogbade, O.M., 1982. 'Livestock development and range use in Nigeria', in J.G. Galaty (ed.), *The Future of Pastoral Peoples*. International Development Centre: Ottawa.

Awogbade, O.M. and Famoriyo, S., 1982. *Nomadic Land Use and Beef Production in Nigeria*. Proceedings of the Conference on Beef Production in Nigeria, Ahmadu. Bello University Press: Zaria.

Beckman, B., 1985. 'Neo-colonialism, capitalism and the state in Nigeria', in H. Bernstein and B.K. Capmbell (eds), *Contradictions of Accumulation in Africa*, Sage: Beverly Hills.

Beckman, B., 1987. 'Public investment and agrarian transformation in northern Nigeria', in M. Watt, *State, Oil and Agriculture in Nigeria*. Institute of International Studies. University of California: Berkeley.

Bryson, R., 1973. *The Sahelian Effect*. University of Wisconsin Press: Madison.

Derrick, J., 1977. 'The great West African drought', *African Affairs*, no. 76.

Derrick, J., 1984. 'West Africans' worst year of famine', *African Affairs*, no. 83.

Franke, R.W. and Chasin, B., 1980. *Seeds of Famine: Ecological Destruction and the Development Dilemma in West African Sahel*. Montlair: London.

Galal el-Din, 1974. 'The Factor Influencing Migration to the Three Towns of the Sudan'. *Sudan Journal of Economic and Social Studies*, vol. 1, no. 1.

George, S., 1984. *Ill Fares the Land: Essays on Food, Hunger and Power*. Institute for Policy Studies: Washington DC.

Hassan, U.A., 1987. *The River Basin Development Strategy and the Integration of Pastoral Fulbe.* MSc. Zaria, unpublished thesis, Ahmadu Bello University.

Hinderink, J. and Sterkenburg, J.J., 1987. *Agricultural Commercialization and Government Policy in Africa.* KPI: London and New York.

Ibrahim, F.N., 1978. *The Problem of Desertification in the Republic of the Sudan with Special Reference to Northern Dar Fur Province.* Khartoum University Press: Khartoum.

Ibrahim, F.N., 1984. *Ecological Imbalance in the Republic of the Sudan.* Brockhaus Bayreuth Verlagsgesellaschaft: Bayreuth.

Ihonvbere, J.O. and Shaw, T.M., 1988. *Towards a Political Economy of Nigeria.* Avebury: Aldershot.

Kadouf, H. and Mohamed Salih, M.A., 1986. *Land Tenure and Rural Development in the Southern Kordofan.* Sudan Ministry of Planning: Khartoum.

Michael, H.G. et. al. (eds), 1987. *Drought and Hungar in Africa.* Cambridge University Press: Cambridge.

Mohamed Salih, M.A., 1987. 'The tractor and the plough: the sociological dimension', in M.A. Mohamed Salih (ed.), *Agrarian Change in the Central Rainlands* Sudan. Scandinavian Institute of African Studies: Sudan, Uppsala.

Mohamed Salih, M.A., 1989. 'Ecological degradation, political coercion and the limits of state intervention, Sudan', in Anders Hjort af Ornäs and M. A. Mohamed Salih (eds), *Ecology and Politics: Environmental Crisis and Security in Africa.* Scandinavian Institute of African Studies: Uppsala.

Mohamed Salih, M.A., 1989. 'The response of agropastoralists to the state agricultural policies, the predicament of the Baggara, Western Sudan'. A paper presented to the Workshop on Adaptive Strategies in African Arid Lands. Scandinavian Institute of African Studies: Uppsala.

Nnoli, O., 1989. 'Desertification, refugees and regional conflicts in West Africa', in Anders Hjort af Ornäs and M.A. Mohamed Salih (eds), *Ecology and Politics: Environmental Stress and Security in Africa.* Scandinavian Institute of African Studies: Uppsala.

O'Brien, J., 1978. 'How traditional is traditional agriculture in Sudan', *Journal of Economic and Social Studies,* vol. 2, no. 1. Previously issued as ESRC Bulletin no. 62. Khartoum: Economic and Social Research Council, (1977).

Okaiyeto, P.O., 1982. Livestock Development Strategies in Nigeria, in the Proceedings of the Conference on Beef Production in Nigeria. Ahmadu Bello University: Zaria.

Rasmusson, M. Eugene, 1987. 'Global climate change and variability: effects on drought and desertification in Africa', in Michael H. Glants (ed.), *Drought and Hunger in Africa: Denying Famine a Future.* Cambridge University Press: London.

Rotberg, R.I. (ed.), 1983. *Imperialism, Colonialism and Hunger: East and Central Africa.* Lexington Books: London.

Saeed, M.H., 1982. 'Economic effects of agricultural mechanization in rural

Sudan', in G. Haaland (ed.), *Problems of Savannah Development, the Case of Sudan.* Bergen Occasional Papers in Social Anthropology no. 19, Bergen.

Sen, A., 1981. *Poverty and Famine.* Oxford University Press: London.

Shenton, R., 1986. *The Development of Capitalism in Northern Nigeria.* James Currey: London.

Spooner, P. and Mann, H.S. (eds), 1982. *Desertification and Development in Dry Ecology in Social Perspective.* Academic Press: New York.

Timberlake, L., 1984. *Natural Disasters, Acts of God or Acts of Man*, Earthscan: London.

Udo, R.K., 1979. *Geographical Regions of Nigeria.* Heinemann: London.

Wani, P., 1987. 'Poverty versus affluence, the case of Renk District, Southern Sudan', in M.A. Mohamed Salih (ed.), *Agrarian Change in the Central Rainlands, Sudan.* Scandinavian Institute of African Studies: Uppsala.

Watt, M., 1983. *Silent Violence, Food, Famine and Peasantry in Northern Nigeria.* California University Press: Berkeley.

Watt, M., 1987. 'Drought, environment and food security: some reflections on peasants, pastoralists and commercialization in dryland West Africa', in H.G. Michael et al. (eds), *Drought and Hunger in Africa.* Cambridge University Press: Cambridge.

9 Development, Peasants and Environmental Issues in Wollo, Ethiopia

Tuomo Melasuo

1. Introduction

Wollo, one of the northern provinces of Ethiopia, has during the last 20 years become known all over the world as *the* region of famine and drought. There have recently been two serious famines, one in the 1970s and another in 1984–5. A new serious famine was threatening Eritrea, Tigray and the northern part of Wollo in the spring of 1990 and again in the spring 1991.

Yet only a few generations ago Wollo was still quite a prosperous province, producing a good surplus of some importance. Foreign travellers described nineteenth-century Wollo as well-watered, fertile and densely populated (Rubenson, 1988, p. 5). Now the ecological situation of the province is deteriorating significantly, the most important element in this process being land erosion. As to the actual situation in the Wollo highlands, it is estimated that 50% of them are significantly eroded, 25% seriously eroded and 4% beyond any possibility of recovery (Ståhl, 1989, p. 181). The speed of deforestation in Ethiopia has been dramatic in this century. The loss of forest area is estimated to be from an original 40% to 14%, the last figure also including the savannah-type forest, and the share of 'real' forest being only between 3–4%. In Wollo, the forest area has fallen to less than 2% of the total area. If the actual tendency to erosion goes on, one fourth of the present agricultural land will be lost to crop cultivation by the year 2010 (Ståhl, 1989, p. 183; Wollo Profile, 1988, pp. 7 and 74).

Since the revolution of 1974 the regime which was destituted in May 1991 tried to change the general situation in rural areas by introducing a land reform programme which first of all put an end to all kinds of 'feudal' structures in the countryside. Further, the revolutionary government tried to improve rural life by reorganizing the whole system of agricultural production and its socio-political structures.

This was done by creating the so-called Peasant Associations (PAs) as basic units of production, as well as by encouraging the formation of Service Cooperatives and Producer Cooperatives. One of the main tasks of the PAs was the distribution of agricultural and grazing land among its members. Before May 1991, the PAs regrouped 83% of the rural population in Wollo—consisting of more than 2.8 million people— which is 661,000 Wollo families, more or less. The service cooperatives were formed by 448,000 families, which was 56% of the rural population, but the producer Cooperatives covered only 4–5% of the peasant families in Wollo (Wollo Profile, 1988, pp. 7 and 103).

In order to feed the urban areas the government introduced the so-called AMC quotas,[1] with fixed cereal prices and production quantities for each peasant family. During the famine years in the 1980s the government introduced a resettlement programme, which had a particularly heavy impact on Wollo; 380,000 out of a total of 600,000 resettled peasants were from this province. This represented almost 11% of the Wollo population (Wollo Profile, 1988, p. 133). They were resettled in the southern provinces of the country. However, the resettlement programme has almost stopped, to be replaced by the so-called villagization programme, with the idea of regrouping dispersed hamlets into new villages close to roads and easy communication facilities.

In general, the main efforts of the previous government's rural and agricultural policies were directed to the southern and western parts of Ehtiopia, which are regarded as surplus-producing areas. Efforts in Tigray and in Wollo have until now been much more modest.

The aim of this chapter is to observe how environmental issues are taken into consideration in a particular forestation programme involving a few PAs south-west of Dessie, the provincial capital of Wollo. We shall try to establish what kind of potential conflicts might be connected with the implementation of the forestation programme. The main ecological problem in this area is land degradation, which is certainly due to long-term climatic changes in that part of Africa. It is, however, also due to human action, which, in the case of Wollo, has for centuries been contributing to the emergence of an ecological catastrophe. In this context many scientists speak of famine, drought and land degradation as manifestations of the historical crisis of agrarian society.

We would like to investigate the nature of the relationship between three different elements: first, the ecological and socio-political realities in the PAs; second, the implication of the development programmes, in this case the forestation project; and, third, the impacts of the government's rural and agricultural policies.

2. Forestation project

The forestation project in question has two main objectives: first, it should produce fuel wood for the population in the towns of Dessie and Kombolcha; second, it should contribute to environmental rehabilitation by improving the state of the vegetation cover in plantation areas and on mountain tops. Further, the forestation project should also provide labour and extra incomes for the rural population of the PAs in the area.

Besides these main goals, which are directly connected to forestation activities, the project should also provide a certain number of community services for the PAs, such as schools, wells and flour mills. In the sphere of forestation the main purpose of the project is to plant several thousand hectares, mainly with *eucalyptus*. Some other trees and plants are also included in the plantation activities, but to a minor degree. The plantations cover the areas of 10 PAs regrouped in two main localities which together comprise 83 traditional hamlets and small villages. Together, these 10 PAs have a population of about 25,000, more than 95% of whom are peasants.

The real role and significance of the forestation project remains as yet unclear. What is the final use of the product? Is the fuel wood sold to the urban population in Dessie and Kombolcha? If the answer is positive, does the local population also have the right of use? What are the rights of the local PAs when the fuel wood plantations belong to the state? These questions, especially when they remain open, affect the possibilities for the integration of the forestation project into the PAs' other activities. In the same way, these questions affect the possibilities for using the forest project effectively for environmental recovery at a local level. The fact that the option of villagization also still remains open for many PAs in the project area does not help. Peasants simply do not know whether they will be living in the same area next year and whether they will be able to use the trees they plant.

3. The impacts of forestation and environmental issues

For several years there have been quite impressive environmental programmes going on in Wollo, conducted by government agencies and NGOs (Non-Governmental Organization), both often funded by foreign donations and aid organizations. The results are said to be remarkable and in a few years green areas have emerged in regions which were already seriously eroded.

The most frequent methods of environmental rehabilitation have been terracing, mountain top and hillsides enclosure, river catchment management and forestation. Terraces have been built over tens of thousands of kilometres in the province, primarily to stop land erosion. There are about 82,000 hectares of mountain tops enclosed in Wollo. Seven large river catchment areas have been included in the rehabilitation programmes and about 15% of their surface has already been 'treated'. The purpose of catchment reorganization is to improve water resource management and its effect on agriculture and the environment.

Concerning forestry activities, it should be noted that about 50 state nurseries have been established in Wollo. Together with the communal nurseries, which are mainly at PA level, they produce about 60 million seedlings a year. This should be enough for the plantation of 25,000 hectares, but the seedlings' survival rate is low: only about 40% in relatively successful cases, and much lower in many others.

Today there are about 140,000 hectares of forest in Wollo. The state forests cover about 46,000 hectares, the natural forests 44,000, and the community forests belonging mainly to the PAs cover about 50,000 hectares. Altogether this is only 1.5–2% of the total area of Wollo (Ståhl, 1989, p. 185; Wollo Profile, 1988, p. 74).

Even if the results of rehabilitation activities have been positive in the environmental context they are far from sufficient. The actual amount of conservation work represented in the above-mentioned figures is not enough to change the degradation tendencies in Wollo. It seems quite clear that environmental conservation and rehabilitation efforts—which are absolutely essential in the worst eroded areas—should be linked with development activities for the rural population in order quantitatively and qualitatively to reach a degree which would be ecologically significant and sustainable. How does this dilemma manifest itself in a forestation project?

The forestation project has diverse impacts, both positive and negative, on its target societies. Here, we will mainly consider the negative impacts in order to find ways of taking them into consideration when planning and implementing such projects in future.

In the *awarjas*[2] west and south-west of Dessie the population density is among the highest in the whole of Ethiopia. The lands are also among the most eroded. In this context the scarcity of land is the biggest problem of the area. There is lack of land for agriculture, for grazing and even for forestation projects. In fact, this lack of land has been the most serious single problem for the forestation project understudy. It has been the most important obstacle to its advance and has forced the project to take on forms not originally planned for or has led to the abandonment of some of the original aims. For instance, a part of the land allocated to forestation has been too eroded even for fuel wood plantation. According to the experts, it should only be used for conservation.

Thus, in fact, the most immediate and the most difficult practical effect of the project in the fields of environmental rehabilitation and forestation is certainly the loss of land previously used by the PAs for other purposes. In the case of the forestation project of our study the land taken has been from 45 to 297 hectares per PA, the average being more than 150 hectares. The percentage of families affected by this land loss varies between 5% and 100% per PA, the average being between 20% and 25%. A total of 1,275 families in 10 PAs have been affected by the forestation project and 400 families have lost both agricultural and grazing land. The loss of land is somewhere between 0.5 and 2.8 hectares per family.

In the case of agricultural land this has meant that the PAs' communal land has been distributed to families who have lost their land or that the PAs have been obliged to make a complete new redistribution involving all of their land.

In particular, the loss of enclosed hillsides is of strategic importance for the peasant population. Traditionally, a peasant family cultivates at least two or even three separated plots which are at different altitudes or of a different kind. This distribution of cultivation makes for diversity and thus anticipates any eventual freak of nature; both drought and frost, the latter being Wollo's most difficult calamity, have different effects at different altitudes. The topographical conditions in which the fields are located determine how sensitive they are to frost. Concentration of cultivation in only one plot will increase the risk of crop failure and is an obstacle to the peasants' survival strategies.

Traditionally, cattle-raising is an important part of agriculture in Wollo. Even today Wollo produces slaughter cattle for Addis Ababa and Asmara. Besides, livestock are less sensitive to climatic changes and to government taxation than agriculture. In the PAs under study the cattle density varies between 12.6 and 48.5 head per hectare. In this context it is clear that the loss of mountain tops and hillsides to forestry constitutes one serious impact of the forestation project. A great number of cattle used to graze on the slopes and mountain tops, especially during the rainy season. Furthermore, it should be noted that these grazing lands now lost to forestation were especially used by the poorest peasants for sheep and goat husbandry. Sheep-raising is often their only hope of 'getting some butter on the bread' and of producing some surplus which can be invested in cattle and later on perhaps in an ox. And in Wollo an ox is an indispensable precondition for effective agriculture.

The loss of grazing land to forestation has had three kinds of impact. First, in some of the PAs the population have been forced to sell their cattle because of the lack of pasture. Second, it has caused serious conflicts between the forestation project and the local population. Third, now that cattle can no longer graze on hillsides they have been moved downwards and this increases ecological stress at the lower altitudes which were formerly used for agriculture in rainy seasons. These problems have made it clear that forage production should be included in forestation and conservation projects.

Apart from the loss of land, the forestation project has also had an impact on the labour situation in its target PAs. A development project can use several hundreds of thousands of man-days of work in its most active periods; for example, the forestry project under study has employed more than 2,200 people a day during its peak periods. Even if the work is paid for in cash or in food-for-work this amount of labour must be taken out of something else. As the agricultural calendar is usually very dependent on the beginning of the rains at very short notice and as oxen availability affects the ideal realization of this calendar, the different work phases of the project should be planned in such a way as not to disturb this very sensitive and vulnerable agricultural calendar. Usually the forestation project has managed to do this as it is only the actual planting phase which must take place at the beginning of the rainy season and which can disturb the PAs' agricultural calendar. But even in this case, it must be noted, the peasants very clearly give priority to their own agricultural activities. If possible, they try to send their wives and children to project work.

The forestation project is a very important source of additional income for the local population and in this sense it can partly compensate for the loss of land. But there are many questions to be answered: How can it be guaranteed that the project does not distort the normal economic life in the area? How can the compensation be controlled so that it has not only a 'monetary' meaning but is also able to give a positive answer to structural changes? How can it be ensured that the project will continue to employ a good number of local people when the peak period is over? What is the relationship between new paid labour and the environmental evolution in the area?

It seems clear that forestation and conservation activities also call for an important measure of development effort in other sectors and even an integrated rural policy on the part of the government in order that their own aims can be realized.

4. Contradictions and politics

In scientific studies it has been estimated that the peasant population of Ethiopia is nowadays an object of more important economic charges than it was before the revolution and the land reform (Dessalegn, 1987, p. 110). In general, the Mengistu government's rural policy was suffering from many handicaps. We can say that rather than its basic orientation it was its method of implementation which was problematic in official rural policy. Often, the methods used were, simply, very authoritative.

An example of this is the way in which the land was allocated to forestation in the project under study. In theory, it is the representatives of the PAs, of the governmental offices and development agencies who should together agree and delimit the land to be given to a forestation project. Often, however, the voice of the PA is not loud enough to stress its point of view sufficiently, and the other two partners are too busy getting on with the practical work. These have also been cases where the land has been agreed on with the PAs on the maps around the desk, but decisions in the field are taken only by government officials, without consultation. The result has been that the land lost has been totally different from what was decided on. In cases like this, is there any kind of planning which could be accepted by the peasants and which could include some environmental issues?

Another example is mountain top and hillside enclosure. The rules and practices of their management have often been criticized in the research literature (Hultin, 1986, pp. 2–3). The areas have usually been enclosed for an unlimited period of time and the authorities do not permit the peasants to use them even in a restricted way. From the point of view of environmental rehabilitation and the development of the wood plantations themselves, a 1–2-year closing would be adequate and reasonable. After this time of absolute closure the animals could resume grazing in the plantation area. When the mountain tops are completely closed the peasants are offered the possibility of gathering fodder by the cut-and-carry method, but the need to transport fodder from the plantation area is time-consuming and hard and therefore unpopular with the peasants. Besides, the fodder should be gathered during the busiest period of the agricultural calendar, at the beginning of the autumn, when its nutritive value is good.

The villagization programme going on in Ethiopia is very much contested by both foreign and national observers. In this case, too, it is the methods which are the most problematic (Faye, 1989): there have been cases in Wollo in which the loss of land to forestation has resulted in the PA in question becoming an object of villagization.

Concerning the 10 PAs of our study, villagization is already being realized in 3 of them; it is actually proceeding in one of the PAs and planned for the near future in another. The destiny of the 5 remaining PAs is still unclear.

The villagization programme has been open to criticism in that one of its negative aspects can be a rapid worsening of the health and food situation when human and cattle populations are living close to each other. It also seems clear that agricultural production might fall off significantly when people are no longer living on their lands, for they often have to walk several kilometres a day in order to reach their plots of land.

The environmental aspects of the villagization programme have not been planned or studied at all. In any case, the construction of thousands of new houses is a stress on the remaining forests of Ethiopia. Moreover, the concentration of human and livestock populations causes a new kind of environmental stress on certain areas.

In evaluating Ethiopia's official rural policy it is very difficult to set a borderline between impacts having environmental importance and those having none. The effects of land reform and the imposition of AMC quotas for the peasant population have been problematic. At the beginning of the land reform AMC quotas could reach 50% of production and as a result there were cases in Wollo in which peasants were obliged to buy cereal on the free markets at treble the price in order to fill their quotas. However, these quotas have been first significantly reduced, especially in Wollo[3] and the whole organization of the AMC was dismantled in spring 1991.

A further controversial aspect of official rural policy is created by the producer cooperatives, which seem only to serve outside markets and the needs of the government. Usually, membership of these cooperatives is voluntary, but sometimes only the young and wealthy can join and only members of a cooperative can take advantage of certain technological innovations and financial facilities offered by the government. It also happens that financial resources are collected from *all* peasants in the area while only producer cooperative-members can have the use of them. Further, it has been claimed that the cooperatives have appropriated the best land and in unequally large proportions compared to the standards of the PA in question. Sometimes the cooperatives simply do not have enough resources to cultivate all the lands they collect. From this point of view it does not appear at all certain that in the long run social and economic equality is increasing in the Ethiopian countryside (Pausewang, 1988, pp. 142–4).

In order to have a real dynamic rural policy with any prospect of resolving the main problems in the countryside, much more attention needs to be paid to the roles of the local PAs. When planning development activities or general options of rural policy, more account should be taken of the 'autonomous' development processes going on in rural areas and in PAs. The integration of the PAs and their specificities to activities should be improved and planned with care, especially with regard to the environment.

The environmental situation in Wollo and in many other parts of Ethiopia is so difficult that the full contribution of the peasant societies is absolutely essential. The Ethiopian government and foreign aid agencies cannot hope to reverse the tendency to environmental degradation (Ståhl, 1989, p. 181) without the active participation of the peasants.

To induce the peasants, who are fully aware of the environmental problems of their lands, to take charge of their rehabilitation requires a change of attitude in the government's rural policy. There is a need to reduce authoritarianism and to improve democracy, especially for the peasants to organize their own life and production. Such democratization is essential in order to create a development process which could permit environmental rehabilitation in Ethiopian countryside.

However, the new provisional government, which has just emerged from a serious and difficult civil war in Eritrea, in Tigray and even in Wollo, has a lot of difficulties to change the rural policies rapidly. But the process which is conducive to peace and the end of the war situation can create the conditions in which a democratization of rural policy would be possible. This is a precondition for all long-term conservation and environmental rehabilitation activities as well as for rural development at least in the northern part of Ethiopia.

Even if there has been the end of the war in May 1991, the overall situation is far from easy or promising. The old government had announced some major changes in internal order in March 1990, and the new provisional government is planning for general elections in the coming two years. But whether this is really also leading to a process of democratization in rural areas remains unclear.

Notes

1. AMC Agricultural Marketing Corporation, was a state agency purchasing the agricultural production from the peasant population. AMC quotas were abolished in March 1990 and in spring 1991 it totally stopped its activities.
2. *Awaraja*, one of the administrative units in Ethiopia.
3. As noted, the AMC quotas were abolished in March 1990.

References

Ege, Svein (ed.), 1988. *Development in Ethiopia*. Working Paper on Ethiopian Development, no. 3, University of Trondheim.

Dessalegn, Rahmato, 1987. *Famine and Survival Strategies. A Case Study from Northeastern Ethiopia*. Food and Famine Monograph Series no. 1, Institute of Development Research, Addis Ababa University.

Faye, Bernard, 1989. 'Ethiopie, la logique de la villagisation', *Le Monde Diplomatique*, Paris, April.

Hultin, Jan, 1986. 'The predicament of the peasants in conservation-based development', *SIDA Support to Welo Region*. Background Papers. Stockholm.

Melasuo, Tuomo and Worko, Amare, 1990. *Peasant Association Study in Wollo, Ethiopia*, Tapri, Occasional Papers no. 42, Tampere.

Pausewang, Siegfried, 1988. 'Peasants, organisations, markets: ten years after the land reform', in Ege, Svein (ed.) *Development in Ethiopia*. Working Papers on Ethiopian Development, no. 3, University of Trondheim.

Rubenson, Sven, 1988. 'Conflict and environmental stress in Ethiopian history. Looking for correlations'. Paper to Conference on Environmental Stress and Security, Stockholm, 13–15 December.

Ståhl, Michael, 1989. 'Environmental and political constraints in Ethiopia', in Anders Hjort af Ornäs and M.A. Mohamed Salih (eds), *Ecology and Politics*. Scandinavian Institute of African Studies: Uppsala.

Wollo Profile, 1988. Addis Ababa.

10 The Concept of Security — From Limited to Comprehensive

Jyrki Käkönen

1. Traditional security

The concept of security is easily perceived as being independent of time and place. It is a general assumption that all states in different historical periods have had a common interest to protect their integrity and independence. As regards the content of security, in political language it means the tasks of a state which attempts to ensure the security of its citizens against outside threats. It is in this form that it is connected with the real or imaginary security provided by weapons.

It is quite clear, however, that in the historical context the substance of the security concept is connected to the modern international system, which goes back to the early sixteenth century (Modelski, 1983; Hopkins et al. 1982). In other words, it is closely connected to the history of the modern state and the 'anarchic' nature of the international system. There is no reason to speak of security as a collective good provided by states for their citizens before the emergence of modern states.

Before the existence of early modern states the role of armed forces was not exactly to provide protection for people living in a certain specified territory. It is also difficult to speak of security policy in general before the early sixteenth century. In those days the role of armed forces was to protect the power of princes rather than the independence of states or the integrity of a people; armed forces were also used to seize power or capture treasure.

The concept of security was clearly determined by historical development and the determination of the content of the concept meshes seamlessly with the development of nation-states and with competition between states, which has generally been taken for granted. As the state began to be perceived as a sovereign actor in relation to other international actors, it assumed the new function of ensuring the integrity of the territory and the socio-political organization of the state. This development took place as late as the seventeenth and eighteenth centuries. Up to the early nineteenth century, along with states, there were other international actors, such as pirates and privateers who were able to use armed force.

Regional and organizational integrity meant that actors defined as outsiders had no right to interfere in the internal affairs of states. In the end, any attempt to interfere had to be prevented, if need be by armed force. This responsibility was already given to the modern state by Niccolo Machiavelli, the father of the traditional theory of international politics. Machiavelli wanted a united Italian state strong enough to prevent France and Spain from annexing Italian territories.

In the theories of Machiavelli and Hobbes the maintenance of organized state power had an essential position, in that it guaranteed the internal peace and security of any society. The integrity of inhabitants or citizens has always been subordinated to the integrity of the state. In principle, borders have been protected to ward off any physical threat to the citizens, but in practice human sacrifices have been accepted in order to save the state. In this line of argument, which can be connected to Hegel, the state is something greater and more sacred than the citizens or civil society which form it.

The historical connections of security policy in themselves imply the possibility that the state and its citizens may see security threats differently. And even if this were not the case, the content of the concept is today changing as regards citizens' threat images. Various international and national opinion polls have shown that fear of war and armed attack are not necessarily the most central threat images in people's minds. Nevertheless, almost 20% of the wealth attained yearly by humankind is still being used for preventing armed threats (Renner, 1989, pp. 14–24). Allocation of social resources in this way is possible only by creating and maintaining enemy images.

In opinion polls the insecurity felt by people and their threat images are connected with factors like the possible overpopulation of the world and thereby a marked deterioration in the preconditions for existence; the exhaustion of natural resources in increasing the standard of living and making the international community more equal; hunger as the area under cultivation becomes smaller and the productivity of the oceans diminishes; the threat of an ecocatastrophe or the greenhouse effect connected with ozone layer thinning, and new diseases such as AIDS, for which there is as yet no remedy (Hettne, 1984, pp. 100–2).

The above list is problematic because all the new threats are connected—just as armed security is—with the form of social and economic organization in which we, the rich of the northern hemisphere, live. Underdevelopment and the phenomena connected with it, as well as environmental problems, are phenomena of destruction caused by development. In other words, different threats are closely connected to a set of values and way of life, which in the end constitute a threat to continuity. And together these phenomena are part and parcel of the crisis of the modernization project.

In today's world it is difficult to differentiate between the factors of threat. At the same time, we have to note that it is just as difficult to admit that they are concealed in our own activities. Yet it may be necessary to admit this. When exercising authority and distributing socialized resources to strengthen the security of citizens and to solve problems, we have to choose between different threat images. Roughly speaking, the decision has to be made between traditional security and other factors threatening security.

The solution of the foregoing problem, connected as it is with the dialectics of development and destruction, has to be regarded as one of the key questions in current security—political discussion. A decision has to be made between the values and groups of people connected with the modernization project and on the other hand between the needs and the objectives of the majority of humankind. So far, security policy has been dominated by the preferences of those in power (Ylikangas, 1986, pp. 251–9). Social resources are redistributed with the emphasis on armed security. Considerably fewer resources have been sacrificed to the solution of other security-threatening problems. Altogether less than 2% of the yearly global GNP is used to solve the development and environmental problems of our globe (Renner, 1989, pp. 25–46).

Setting the preferences in the above way is closely connected with the threat images of social powers. In addition to the prevention of external threat, the fear of losing status has a central position in them. The insufficiency of social resources in the great projects, which were created by so-called affluent society and by which the people's rights to education, health service or social security were protected, reflect threats that concern the continuity of society (Sipilä, 1985, pp. 15–32, 89–106; Käköen, 1986). The possibility of increasing inequality raises threats which are faced by the affluent elites and by forces bound to the continuity of the modern state and existing social structures.

The above-mentioned insufficiency adds to the internal threats in society. Displacement and the weakening of social security gives rise to violence, which is easily manifested in racial hatred and which in our time has also shown itself in football violence (Käkönen, 1986, 31; Hietanen, 1986). Violence always increases the threat to the legitimacy of the system, and to prevent it an element of armed security is needed. Thus, armament functions are a mechanism by which both the status of ruling social groups is protected and resources are allocated to their use (Ylikangas, 1986, pp. 255–6; Renner, 1989, p. 60).

2. Extending the concept of security

Armament is not, however, a sufficient answer to the solution of the problems. It seems rather that it eats into the resources that would be needed to eliminate other problems and factors threatening security. This kind of connection has already led to a revaluation of the concept of security and its considerable expansion.

We have moved towards the expansion of the concept of security on a variety of activity levels. In the minds of citizens the concept has expanded in face of new threat images. Modern communication has made these threat images everyday reality to 'ordinary' people. Among researchers the concept has also acquired new content. This kind of change in content also shows in research analyses connected with the traditional theory of international politics. Many representatives of the realist school consider new aspects of security together with armed security; the most prominent of these is possibly environmental security (Buzan, 1989).

The influence of the foregoing quarters on everyday international politics is not, however, always direct. Therefore, as regards the change and expansion of the concept, it is important that many international expert bodies redefined security as far back as the late 1970s and more especially in the 1980s. The following expert bodies should be mentioned in particular: the commission on North–South relations under the direction of Willy Brandt, former Federal Chancellor of the FRG; the commission on international disarmament and security under the direction of Olof Palme, late Prime Minister of Sweden; the commission on development and armament under the direction of Inga Thorson, a Swedish minister for disarmament; and the commission on environmental questions under the direction of Gro Harlem Brundtland, Prime Minister of Norway.

Regarding the problem under discussion, all these reports have in common the connection of armament to poverty and hunger in the world. Both phenomena, according to the reports, increase the probability of conflicts, which maintains the need for armament. The problems form a vicious circle, in which they feed each other while the increase in the amount of weapons ultimately adds to insecurity in the international community. In other words, armed security works against its own original goal, so that armament has become a central source of insecurity—a threat to humankind.

It is quite evident that the definition of the concept of security in solely military terms is highly problematic in the era of interdependence. Concentration on the military element easily transforms economy into a strategic element. This leads to a situation where the guaranteeing of economic security becomes a military problem and no longer a political or purely economic one. This transforms distant economic interests such as Persian Gulf oil into elements of national security for states depending on imported oil. Trade will lose its original essence as an instrument moving economic values between societies and states. Finally, economic interdependence or distant security threats in economy will get military solutions (Käkönen, 1987, pp. 115–19). This development is sufficient reason for defining the concept of security in a broader sense than has traditionally been the case.

3. Environmental problems and security

As regards the use of resources, environmental problems offer perhaps the best example of the difference between traditional security–political thinking and comprehensive security–political thinking. Even now, environmental changes affect the relations between people, social groups, ethnic groups and states. In the arid areas of the earth people even now have to resolve the conflict between different modes of production, for example in relation to the right to use water (Chapter 8 in this book; Sarmela, 1988, pp. 129–33).

This conflict often arises between ethnic communities and it therefore also leads to ethnic conflicts (Chapters 7 and 8 in this book). Environmental changes are growing into a factor which will in the future possibly cause the greatest numbers of refugees. In international practice environmental refugees do not, however, meet the requirements set for the definition of a refugee. And neither does one, therefore, need to apply the same rules to them as to political refugees. Environmental changes and refugees cause together and separately open violence and conflicts. This has already happened in the resettlement projects in Ethiopia (Arsano, 1989).

In order to solve environmental conflicts many states arm themselves. In other words, states still prepare to defend themselves by force of arms against any kind of threat. At the same time it can be clearly shown that the resources used for armaments run counter to the solution of the problems creating the need for armament. If resources were used to tackle environmental problems, some of the factors that perpetuate the need for armament would be eliminated. According to this view, security may be produced as a common good and, in the broad sense of the concept, for citizens in many states. Thus, comprehensive security may also be called collective security in a more diverse sense than before.

As regards the international system, or perhaps it would be more proper to say as regards the international community, environmental changes ought to be regarded as serious factors threatening the security of the community. During the history of humankind, environmental changes have affected both states and the power relations between states. And the reactions to changes of this kind have often been the use of force (Harris, 1982). As traditional security–political thinking maintains its ruling status, it is not difficult to imagine that states would still solve even problems caused by environmental changes by resorting to force. Despite disarmament efforts, states have not dissociated themselves from the policy of using force as their ultimate means of resolving conflicts, and the development of new arms technology has not yet ceased.

In Europe, the migrations of peoples used to be one of the factors causing the breakup of the old system. Behind these migrations were growth of population, environmental changes and expectations of a 'higher standard of living'. These same factors can already be found behind extensive emigrations in the international system. And it is to be expected that the largest emigrations in history are still to come if the greenhouse effect comes true at least in accordance with the 'second worst' alternative, in other words even if the worst predictions remained only utopias of fear. And as a result of large-scale emigration there would no longer be borders separating nations and so-called nation-states. There will only be multinational and multiethnic societies. Such prospects turn arguments away from the traditional security policy.

It has been estimated that the greenhouse effect will raise the sea level by one meter, for example in the Indian Ocean, after the year 2000. This would mean that for instance the Maldive Islands would be left under water. This would be no great problem because of the small population. A real problem would be created by Bangladesh, which even today is flooded each year and in which maybe a couple of hundred million people would be left homeless. These people would have to settle somewhere, or one answer to their migration might be resort to force.

The use of force as a security–political means of solving environmental problems may seem to be unnecessary denigration. This is not so, however, if the problem is approached in terms of another, new threat image. During the last few years drugs have come to be perceived as a factor seriously threatening at least Western societies and states. The prevention of this threat may be compared to the traditional security policy in that so far it has sought to prevent the threat mainly at state borders.

For various reasons the borders have remained leaky and drugs have been transported in great quantities. Now, and especially in the summer of 1989, the threat has come to be countered outside the borders of states under threat by the traditional security–political means, i.e. military power. This viewpoint is clearly included in the anti-drug war program of US President George Bush (USIS, (United States Information Service) 7 September 1989).

If traditional armed security policy is used as a means in the anti-drug 'war', it is not far-fetched to imagine it being equally used in threatening situations caused by environmental changes. In a situation where the use of military power in the traditional sense does not seem so necessary any longer, the need for armament and the maintenance of power may be explained by new threats. This is done because military power is still an important means of preserving the current power structures.

As regards the subject under consideration, it is essential to note that in fighting drugs the resources allocated to the use of force are deficited from the actual solutions to the problem. In this respect the situation is comparable to the environmental problem. Most primary producers of drugs—farmers—produce them because the income earned from them may be the only alternative to or it exceeds the income earned from other agricultural products (Kawell, 1989, pp. 25–38). If the same producers were paid proper compensation for other agricultural products, the production of drugs would no longer be profitable. In other words, if funds were used in advance to fight poverty, it would reduce the subsequent need to use funds to fight the production of and international trade in drugs.

Understanding the problems in the way described above, we realize that it is not possible to increase security in the context of traditional values and within the framework of existing economic and political structures. And those social actors who benefit from the existing structures and processes will certainly be ready, at least still in the near future, to maintain their privileges even by force. Therefore, any kind of long-term security in the international system will entail a peaceful transformation of the whole international system.

As this possible future is studied in the framework of limited and comprehensive security policy, it becomes clear that resources would be more wisely employed to face the environmental problem or the drug problem now than to answer by traditional coercive means the threat they entail in the future. An attempt to eliminate the problem now strengthens security in the future. But no such decision has yet been made. When state resources are redistributed, the focus has remained the same. If the situation were different, armament would not get, as mentioned, almost a fifth of all the value produced by humankind every year.

4. Security of civil society

I have chosen this mode of examination to prove that the traditional emphasis on national security is an outdated conception. We have to be able to move from national security to global security, where the starting-point is not the survival of separate states and political systems but the survival of all humankind and the environment it needs. Hopes of a change of this kind are included in the international politics of our time.

In 1987 the General Assembly of the United Nations introduced the concept of environmental security. And in connection with the new initiative-taking in international politics Mr Gorbachev has introduced the concept of economic security. Both these expansions work purposefully towards a comprehensive concept of security.

On the basis of the comprehensive concept of security policy, there is no such sufficient defence in which the amount of weapons would be decisive. And the same conclusion has to be drawn on the basis of the limited concept of security as well. The more military power a state has, the more insecure the areas surrounding it will feel in the international system, which is imagined to be anarchistic and which is filled with suspicion. Therefore, maximum armed security of one state leads to the armament of others, and at the same time maximum security becomes relative.

When thinking of the factors of threat and problem solution in the context of the comprehensive concept of security in relation to armed security, we see that the maintenance of armed security detracts from the preconditions for a solution to other threats. At the same time we note that armed defense and its maintenance always means defense of the prevailing conditions. In other words, as the emphasis remains on armed security–political solutions, we may assume that there is no real will in the international system to solve problems people perceive as threats to themselves.

When this problem is approached from another direction, we may come to the conclusion that a secure world is a world where one need not feel the fears connected with the system. This again means that security is increased by making the relations between people more equal and rendering decision-making in the international community more democratic. As to the realization of these comprehensive objectives of humankind, it maintains that the resources created by humankind are not used on weapons but the environment. The environment is today a public good more than is traditional armed security in the framework of nation-states.

In this chapter I have posed a viewpoint according to which the security–political interests of states and their citizens are not necessarily convergent in our world. This conclusion may be reframed by saying that the security–political interest of nation-state and that of civil society are in conflict. And if the conflict is reduced to a dichotomy, the traditional nation-state security policy has to be regarded as a threat from the viewpoint of civil society.

Still holding to this strict dichotomic interpretation, we come to the interesting conclusion that any strategy or political action against a nation-state has to be considered to be one dimension of security policy. This may be logically argued to mean that as nation-states become less important, the basis of armed security also narrows (Hettne, 1984), provided, of course, that the security of other possible forms of social organization is not also based on weapons.

Of course a pessimistic viewpoint is not unfounded, but its likelihood is the smaller the more clearly the security of a civil society is defined in terms of the new factors of threat presented in this study. The pessimistic possibility is also reduced by the fact that as a forum of self-management of citizens a civil society takes on more and more tasks belonging to a centralized state system. At the same time civil societies have to create forms of international organization and administrative institutions that go beyond the relationships between states. If civil societies develop in this direction and their importance as an area of autonomy for citizens grows, we may assume that in the international system we are moving from the military alliances formed by nation-states to environmental alliances (Renner, 1989, p. 64) which are formed by civil societies and whose task is to ensure security on the basis of the comprehensive concept of security.

Lastly, however, it is important to deny the presence of an absolute dichotomy in the interests of nation-states and civil societies. Taking into consideration the very short history of nation-states in most parts of the world, it is unlikely that they will disappear soon. Nevertheless the importance of civil societies will probably grow at the expense of nation-states. In this process the civil society in this historical era has to be seen mainly as a means of changing states and their role. And in the process of change the tasks of states as well as the content of security policy will be redefined.

References

Arsano, J., 1989. The argument is based on a discussion with Dr Yacob Arsano in Teheran.

Buzan, Barry, 1989. 'The systemic context of European security'. Working Papers, no. 5. Centre for Peace and Conflict Research: Copenhagen.

Harris, Marvin, 1982. *Kulttuurien synty*. Kirjayhtymä: Vaasa.

Hettne, Björn, 1984. 'Approaches to the study of peace and development. A state of the art report'. EADI, Working Paper, no. 6, August.

Hietanen, Aki, 1986. 'Urheilun katsomoväkivalta: ilmiön urheilukeskeisistä ja yhteiskunnallisista selvityksistä', *Rauhantutkimus*, no. 2.

Hopkins, Terence K. et al., 1982. 'Cyclic rythms and secular trends of the capitalist world economy: some premises, hypotheses and questions', in Terence Hopkins and Immanuel Wallerstein et al. (eds), *World-System Analysis. Theory and Methodology*. Sage: Beverly Hills.

Kawell, Jo Ann, 1989. 'Under the Flag of Law Enforcement' and 'The Addict Economics', in *NACLA Reports on the Americas*, vol. 22, no. 6.

Käkönen, Jyrki, 1986. 'Scarcity and violence', *Current Research on Peace and Violence*, vol. 9, no. 3.

Käkönen, Jyrki, 1987. 'The politics of scarcity in the changing world system: implications for Europe', in Vilho Harle (ed.), *Challenges and Responses in European Security*. Avebury: Aldershot.

Modelski, George, 1983. 'Long cycles of world leadership', in William R. Thompson (ed.), *Contending Approaches to World System Analysis*. Sage: Beverly Hills.

Renner, Michael, 1989. 'National security: the economic and environmental dimensions'. Worldwatch Paper, no. 89. May.

Sarmela, Matti, 1988. *Paikalliskulttuurin rakennemuutos*. Karisto Oy: Hämeenlinna.

Sipilä, Jorma, 1985. *Sosiaalipolitiikan tulevaisuus*. Tammi: Helsinki.

Yhteinen tulevaisuutemme (Our Common Future), 1988. Report of the World Commission on Environment and Development. Valtion Painatuskeskus: Helsinki.

Ylikangas, Heikki, 1986. *Käännekohtia Suomen historiassa*. WSOY: Juva.

USIS, 1989. Official text, 7 September. United States Information Service.

Index